MASTER THE™ DSST®

Health and Human Development Exam

About Peterson's

Peterson's® has been your trusted educational publisher for over 50 years. It's a milestone we're quite proud of, as we continue to offer the most accurate, dependable, high-quality educational content in the field, providing you with everything you need to succeed. No matter where you are on your academic or professional path, you can rely on Peterson's for its books, online information, expert test-prep tools, the most up-to-date education exploration data, and the highest quality career success resources—everything you need to achieve your education goals. For our complete line of products, visit **www.petersons.com.**

For more information, contact Peterson's, 4380 S. Syracuse Street, Suite 200, Denver CO 80237; 800-338-3282 Ext. 54229; or find us online at **www.petersons.com**.

Contents

Before You Begin

HOW THIS BOOK IS ORGANIZED

Peterson's *Master*™ *the DSST Health and Human Development* provides a diagnostic test, subject-matter review, and a post-test.

- **Diagnostic Test**—Twenty multiple-choice questions, followed by an answer key with detailed answer explanations
- **Assessment Grid**—A chart designed to help you identify areas that you need to focus on based on your test results
- **Subject-Matter Review**—General overview of the exam subject, followed by a review of the relevant topics and terminology covered on the exam
- **Post-test**—Sixty multiple-choice questions, followed by an answer key and detailed answer explanations

The purpose of the diagnostic test is to help you figure out what you know—or don't know. The twenty multiple-choice questions are similar to the ones found on the DSST exam, and they should provide you with a good idea of what to expect. Once you take the diagnostic test, check your answers to see how you did. Included with each correct answer is a brief explanation regarding why a specific answer is correct, and in many cases, why other options are incorrect. Use the assessment grid to identify the questions you miss so that you can spend more time reviewing that information later. As with any exam, knowing your weak spots greatly improves your chances of success.

Following the diagnostic test is a subject-matter review. The review summarizes the various topics covered on the DSST exam. Key terms are defined; important concepts are explained; and when appropriate, examples are provided. As you read the review, some of the information may seem familiar while other information may seem foreign. Again, take note of the unfamiliar because that will most likely cause you problems on the actual exam.

After studying the subject-matter review, you should be ready for the post-test. The post-test contains sixty multiple-choice items, and it will serve as a dry run for the real DSST exam. There are complete answer explanations at the end of the test.

OTHER DSST® PRODUCTS BY PETERSON'S

Books, flashcards, practice tests, and videos available online at **www.petersons.com/testprep/dsst**

- A History of the Vietnam War
- Art of the Western World
- Astronomy
- Business Mathematics
- Business Ethics and Society
- Civil War and Reconstruction
- Computing and Information Technology
- Criminal Justice
- Environmental Science
- Ethics in America
- Ethics in Technology
- Foundations of Education
- Fundamentals of College Algebra
- Fundamentals of Counseling
- Fundamentals of Cybersecurity
- General Anthropology
- Health and Human Development
- History of the Soviet Union
- Human Resource Management

- Introduction to Business
- Introduction to Geography
- Introduction to Geology
- Introduction to Law Enforcement
- Introduction to World Religions
- Lifespan Developmental Psychology
- Math for Liberal Arts
- Management Information Systems
- Money and Banking
- Organizational Behavior
- Personal Finance
- Principles of Advanced English Composition
- Principles of Finance
- Principles of Public Speaking
- Principles of Statistics
- Principles of Supervision
- Substance Abuse
- Technical Writing

Like what you see? Get unlimited access to Peterson's full catalog of DSST practice tests, instructional videos, flashcards, and more for **75% off the first month!** Go to **www.petersons.com/testprep/dsst** and use coupon code **DSST2020** at checkout. Offer expires July 1, 2021.

Chapter 1

All About the DSST® Exam

WHAT IS DSST®?

Previously known as the DANTES Subject Standardized Tests, the DSST program provides the opportunity for individuals to earn college credit for what they have learned outside of the traditional classroom. Accepted or administered at more than 1,900 colleges and universities nationwide and approved by the American Council on Education (ACE), the DSST program enables individuals to use the knowledge they have acquired outside the classroom to accomplish their educational and professional goals.

WHY TAKE A DSST® EXAM?

DSST exams offer a way for you to save both time and money in your quest for a college education. Why enroll in a college course in a subject you already understand? For more than 30 years, the DSST program has offered the perfect solution for individuals who are knowledgeable in a specific subject and want to save both time and money. A passing score on a DSST exam provides physical evidence to universities of proficiency in a specific subject. More than 1,900 accredited and respected colleges and universities across the nation award undergraduate credit for passing scores on DSST exams. With the DSST program, individuals can shave months off the time it takes to earn a degree.

The DSST program offers numerous advantages for individuals in all stages of their educational development:

- Adult learners
- College students
- Military personnel

Adult learners desiring college degrees face unique circumstances—demanding work schedules, family responsibilities, and tight budgets. Yet adult learners also have years of valuable work experience that can frequently be applied toward a degree through the DSST program. For example, adult learners with on-the-job experience in business and management might be able to skip the Business 101 courses if they earn passing marks on DSST exams such as Introduction to Business and Principles of Supervision.

Adult learners can put their prior learning into action and move forward with more advanced course work. Adults who have never enrolled in a college course may feel a little uncertain about their abilities. If this describes your situation, then sign up for a DSST exam and see how you do. A passing score may be the boost you need to realize your dream of earning a degree. With family and work commitments, adult learners often feel they lack the time to attend college. The DSST program provides adult learners with the unique opportunity to work toward college degrees without the time constraints of semester-long course work. DSST exams take two hours or less to complete. In one weekend, you could earn credit for multiple college courses.

The DSST exams also benefit students who are already enrolled in a college or university. With college tuition costs on the rise, most students face financial challenges. The fee for each DSST exam starts at $85 (plus administration fees charged by some testing facilities)—significantly less than the $750 average cost of a 3-hour college class. Maximize tuition assistance by taking DSST exams for introductory or mandatory course work. Once you earn a passing score on a DSST exam, you are free to move on to higher-level course work in that subject matter, take desired electives, or focus on courses in a chosen major.

Not only do college students and adult learners profit from DSST exams, but military personnel reap the benefits as well. If you are a member of the armed services at home or abroad, you can initiate your post-military career by taking DSST exams in areas with which you have experience. Military personnel can gain credit anywhere in the world, thanks to the fact that almost all of the tests are available through the internet at designated testing locations. DSST testing facilities are located at more than 500 military installations, so service members on active duty can get a jump-start on a post-military career with the DSST program. As an additional incentive, DANTES (Defense Activity for Non-Traditional Education Support) provides funding for DSST test fees for eligible members of the military.

More than 30 subject-matter tests are available in the fields of Business, Humanities, Math, Physical Science, Social Sciences, and Technology.

Available DSST® Exams

Business	Social Sciences
Business Ethics and Society	A History of the Vietnam War
Business Mathematics	Art of the Western World
Computing and Information Technology	Criminal Justice
Human Resource Management	Foundations of Education
Introduction to Business	Fundamentals of Counseling
Management Information Systems	General Anthropology
Money and Banking	History of the Soviet Union
Organizational Behavior	Introduction to Geography
Personal Finance	Introduction to Law Enforcement
Principles of Finance	Lifespan Developmental Psychology
Principles of Supervision	Substance Abuse
	The Civil War and Reconstruction

Humanities	Physical Sciences
Ethics in America	Astronomy
Introduction to World Religions	Environmental Science
Principles of Advanced English Composition	Health and Human Development
Principles of Public Speaking	Introduction to Geology

Math	Technology
Fundamentals of College Algebra	Ethics in Technology
Math for Liberal Arts	Fundamentals of Cybersecurity
Principles of Statistics	Technical Writing

As you can see from the table, the DSST program covers a wide variety of subjects. However, it is important to ask two questions before registering for a DSST exam.

1. Which universities or colleges award credit for passing DSST exams?
2. Which DSST exams are the most relevant to my desired degree and my experience?

Knowing which universities offer DSST credit is important. In all likelihood, a college in your area awards credit for DSST exams, but find out before taking an exam by contacting the university directly. Then review the list of DSST exams to determine which ones are most relevant to the degree you are seeking and to your base of knowledge. Schedule an appointment with your college adviser to determine which exams best fit your degree program and which college courses the DSST exams can replace. Advisers should also be able to tell you the minimum score required on the DSST exam to receive university credit.

DSST® TEST CENTERS

You can find DSST testing locations in community colleges and universities across the country. Check the DSST website (**www.getcollegecredit. com**) for a location near you or contact your local college or university to find out if the school administers DSST exams. Keep in mind that some universities and colleges administer DSST exams only to enrolled students. DSST testing is available to men and women in the armed services at more than 500 military installations around the world.

HOW TO REGISTER FOR A DSST® EXAM

Once you have located a nearby DSST testing facility, you need to contact the testing center to find out the exam administration schedule. Many centers are set up to administer tests via the internet, while others use printed materials. Almost all DSST exams are available as online tests, but the method used depends on the testing center. The cost for each DSST exam starts at $85, and many testing locations charge a fee to cover their costs for administering the tests. Credit cards are the only accepted payment method for taking online DSST exams. Credit card, certified check, and money order are acceptable payment methods for paper-and-pencil tests.

Test takers are allotted two score reports—one mailed to them and another mailed to a designated college or university, if requested. Online tests generate unofficial scores at the end of the test session, while individuals taking paper tests must wait four to six weeks for score reports.

PREPARING FOR A DSST® EXAM

Even though you are knowledgeable in a certain subject matter, you should still prepare for the test to ensure you achieve the highest score possible. The first step in studying for a DSST exam is to find out what will be on the specific test you have chosen. Information regarding test content is located on the DSST fact sheets, which can be downloaded at no cost from

www.getcollegecredit.com. Each fact sheet outlines the topics covered on a subject-matter test, as well as the approximate percentage assigned to each topic. For example, questions on the Health and Human Development exam are distributed in the following way: Health, wellness, and mind/body connection—20%, Human development and relationships—15%, Addiction—15%, Fitness and nutrition—20%, Risk factors, disease, and disease prevention—20%, and Safety, consumer awareness, and environmental concerns—10%.

In addition to the breakdown of topics on a DSST exam, the fact sheet In addition to the breakdown of topics on a DSST exam, the fact sheet also lists recommended reference materials. If you do not own the recommended books, then check college bookstores. Avoid paying high prices for new textbooks by looking online for used textbooks. Don't panic if you are unable to locate a specific textbook listed on the fact sheet; the textbooks are merely recommendations. Instead, search for comparable books used in university courses on the specific subject. Current editions are ideal, and it is a good idea to use at least two references when studying for a DSST exam. Of course, the subject matter provided in this book will be a sufficient review for most test takers. However, if you need additional information, then it is a good idea to have some of the reference materials at your disposal when preparing for a DSST exam.

Fact sheets include other useful information in addition to a list of reference materials and topics. Each fact sheet includes subject-specific sample questions like those you will encounter on the DSST exam. The sample questions provide an idea of the types of questions you can expect on the exam. Test questions are multiple-choice with one correct answer and three incorrect choices.

The fact sheet also includes information about the number of credit hours ACE has recommended be awarded by colleges for a passing DSST exam score. However, you should keep in mind that not all universities and colleges adhere to the ACE recommendation for DSST credit hours. Some institutions require DSST exam scores higher than the minimum score recommended by ACE. Once you have acquired appropriate reference materials and you have the outline provided on the fact sheet, you are ready to start studying, which is where this book can help.

TEST DAY

After reviewing the material and taking practice tests, you are finally ready to take your DSST exam. Follow these tips for a successful test day experience.

1. **Arrive on time.** Not only is it courteous to arrive on time to the DSST testing facility, but it also allows plenty of time for you to take care of check-in procedures and settle into your surroundings.

2. **Bring identification.** DSST test facilities require that candidates bring a valid government-issued identification card with a current photo and signature. Acceptable forms of identification include a current driver's license, passport, military identification card, or state-issued identification card. Individuals who fail to bring proper identification to the DSST testing facility will not be allowed to take an exam.

3. **Bring the right supplies.** If your exam requires the use of a calculator, you may bring a calculator that meets the specifications. For paper-based exams, you may also bring No. 2 pencils with an eraser and black ballpoint pens. Regardless of the exam methodology, you are NOT allowed to bring reference or study materials, scratch paper, or electronics such as cell phones, personal handheld devices, cameras, alarm wrist watches, or tape recorders to the testing center.

4. **Take the test.** During the exam, take the time to read each question-and-answer option carefully. Eliminate the choices you know are incorrect to narrow the number of potential answers. If a question completely stumps you, take an educated guess and move on—remember that DSSTs are timed; you will have 2 hours to take the exam.

With the proper preparation, DSST exams will save you both time and money. So join the thousands of people who have already reaped the benefits of DSST exams and move closer than ever to your college degree.

HEALTH AND HUMAN DEVELOPMENT EXAM FACTS

The DSST® Health and Human Development exam contains 100 multiple-choice questions that cover human development and relationships; fitness and nutrition; disease and prevention; consumer awareness; psychological disorders and addiction intentional injuries; and violence. Careful reading, critical thinking, and logical analysis will be as important as your knowledge of health-related topics.

Area or Course Equivalent: Health and Human Development
Level: Lower-level baccalaureate
Amount of Credit: 3 Semester Hours
Minimum Score: 400
Source: https://www.getcollegecredit.com/wp-content/assets/factsheets/HealthAndHumanDevelopment.pdf

Below is an outline of what you can expect to be covered on the exam.

I. **Health, Wellness, and Mind/Body Connection—20%**

    a. Dimensions of wellness, health, and lifestyles

    b. Healthy People 2020

    c. Prevention

    d. Mental health and mental illness

II. **Human Development and Relationships—15%**

    a. Reproduction

    b. Sexuality

    c. Intimate relationships

    d. Healthy aging

    e. Death and bereavement

III. **Addiction—15%**

    a. Addictive behavior

    b. Alcohol

    c. Tobacco

    d. Other drugs

    e. Other addictions

IV. **Fitness and Nutrition—20%**

    a. Components of physical fitness

    b. Nutrition and its effect

V. **Risk Factors, Diseases, and Disease Prevention—20%**

    a. Infectious diseases

    b. The cardiovascular system

    c. Types of cancer

    d. Immune disorders

    e. Diabetes, arthritis, and genetic-related disorders

    f. Stress management and coping mechanisms

    g. Common neurological disorders

VI. Safety, Consumer Awareness, and Environmental Concerns—10%

    a. Safety

    b. Intentional injuries and violence

    c. Consumer awareness

    d. Environmental concerns

Chapter 2

Health and Human Development Diagnostic Test

DIAGNOSTIC TEST ANSWER SHEET

1. Ⓐ Ⓑ Ⓒ Ⓓ
2. Ⓐ Ⓑ Ⓒ Ⓓ
3. Ⓐ Ⓑ Ⓒ Ⓓ
4. Ⓐ Ⓑ Ⓒ Ⓓ
5. Ⓐ Ⓑ Ⓒ Ⓓ
6. Ⓐ Ⓑ Ⓒ Ⓓ
7. Ⓐ Ⓑ Ⓒ Ⓓ

8. Ⓐ Ⓑ Ⓒ Ⓓ
9. Ⓐ Ⓑ Ⓒ Ⓓ
10. Ⓐ Ⓑ Ⓒ Ⓓ
11. Ⓐ Ⓑ Ⓒ Ⓓ
12. Ⓐ Ⓑ Ⓒ Ⓓ
13. Ⓐ Ⓑ Ⓒ Ⓓ
14. Ⓐ Ⓑ Ⓒ Ⓓ

15. Ⓐ Ⓑ Ⓒ Ⓓ
16. Ⓐ Ⓑ Ⓒ Ⓓ
17. Ⓐ Ⓑ Ⓒ Ⓓ
18. Ⓐ Ⓑ Ⓒ Ⓓ
19. Ⓐ Ⓑ Ⓒ Ⓓ
20. Ⓐ Ⓑ Ⓒ Ⓓ

HEALTH AND HUMAN DEVELOPMENT DIAGNOSTIC TEST
24 minutes—20 questions

Directions: Carefully read each of the following 20 questions. Choose the best answer to each question and fill in the corresponding circle on the answer sheet. The Answer Key and Explanations can be found following this Diagnostic Test.

---

1. Which of the following is a hereditary condition that causes the body to produce sticky mucus that impairs the lungs and intestinal tract?

   A. Huntington's disease
   B. Achondroplasia
   C. Cystic fibrosis
   D. Hemophilia

2. The highest level in Maslow's Hierarchy of Needs is

   A. social.
   B. physiological needs.
   C. esteem.
   D. self-actualization.

3. An important concept of wellness that involves choosing to focus on only what you can control is

   A. holistic health.
   B. empowerment.
   C. spirituality.
   D. exercise.

4. Which stage of an infection is most contagious?

   A. Incubation
   B. Peak
   C. Recovery
   D. Prodromal

5. Which of the following drugs is classified as an opioid?

   A. Morphine
   B. Marijuana
   C. Phencyclidine
   D. Valium

6. Exercise in which the body supplies oxygen to all body parts
   is called

   A. anaerobic.
   B. isometric.
   C. aerobic.
   D. isokinetic.

7. Which of the following gases has been linked to air pollution and
   damage to the earth's atmosphere?

   A. Hydrogen
   B. Nitrogen
   C. Argon
   D. Methane

8. According to Kubler-Ross, which of the following is the first stage
   in grieving?

   A. Depression
   B. Anger
   C. Denial
   D. Acceptance

9. The hardening of arteries is called

   A. arteriosclerosis.
   B. arthritis.
   C. atherosclerosis.
   D. angina.

10. Which of the following is a characteristic of secondary
    depression?

    A. Onset of depression for no apparent reason
    B. Onset of depression clearly defined by a traumatic event
    C. Depression attributed to brain chemistry
    D. Depression related to insufficient exposure to sunlight

11. Hypertrophic obesity is defined as

    A. the development of more fat cells in babies.
    B. the body's preference to maintain current weight, making it difficult to lose weight.
    C. obesity due to genetic factors.
    D. the growth of fat cells to accommodate increased intake of food.

12. During the transition stage of birth, the

    A. cervix begins to efface.
    B. "bloody show" discharges from vagina.
    C. cervix dilates from seven to ten centimeters.
    D. placenta is delivered.

13. Blood alcohol concentration is influenced by a person's body weight, percentage of body fat, and

    A. the type of drink consumed.
    B. gender.
    C. the amount of food in the stomach.
    D. the time of day.

14. Which type of cancer develops in connective tissue?

    A. Leukemia
    B. Melanoma
    C. Sarcoma
    D. Carcinoma

15. Which statement best describes the difference between barbiturates and tranquilizers?

    A. Barbiturates are addictive, but tranquilizers are not.
    B. Barbiturates cause sleep, and tranquilizers are used to cope during waking hours.
    C. Barbiturates are safe, and tranquilizers are dangerous.
    D. Barbiturates are no longer used, and tranquilizers are widely prescribed.

16. Which of the following is NOT one of the three stages of the GAS theory of stress?

    A. Alarm reaction
    B. Resistance
    C. Distress
    D. Exhaustion

17. Which energy source is most dense and provides stored energy for the body?

    A. Carbohydrates
    B. Vitamins
    C. Fats
    D. Proteins

18. The use of traditional free weights provides which form of exercise?

    A. Isometric
    B. Isotonic
    C. Isokinetic
    D. Aerobic

19. Which of the following can be detected by amniocentesis?

    A. Diabetes
    B. Cleft palate
    C. Down Syndrome
    D. Hemochromatosis

20. Which of the following is NOT a common residential safety principle?

    A. Having a fire escape plan
    B. Changing locks when moving into a new home
    C. Keeping noise at a reasonable level
    D. Asking for identification from strangers such as repairmen

ANSWER KEY AND EXPLANATIONS

1. C	5. A	9. A	13. B	17. C
2. D	6. C	10. B	14. C	18. B
3. B	7. D	11. D	15. B	19. C
4. B	8. C	12. C	16. C	20. C

1. **The correct answer is C.** Cystic fibrosis is a hereditary and often fatal disease that is caused by a genetic mutation. The defective gene causes a deficiency in essential enzymes produced in the pancreas, so the body doesn't properly absorb nutrients. Thick mucus impairs the function of the lungs and intestinal tract. Huntington's disease (choice A) involves a degeneration of cells in certain areas of the brain. Achondroplasia (choice B) is the term used for dwarfism. Hemophilia (choice D) is a genetic disorder in which individuals are missing the factor necessary for blood to clot.

2. **The correct answer is D.** Self-actualization is the highest order according to Abraham Maslow's Hierarchy of Needs. He referred to people who reached this state as *transcenders* and Theory Z people. Self-actualization comes from the need for people to do what they were "meant" to do. Choice A is incorrect because social is the third level of Maslow's Hierarchy. Choice B is incorrect because physiological needs are the first level in the Hierarchy of Needs. Choice C is incorrect because esteem for self and others is the fourth level of the hierarchy.

3. **The correct answer is B.** Empowerment is choosing to focus on controlling only that which you have power over. Holistic health (choice A) focuses on taking care of your physical, psychological, social, intellectual, and spiritual self. Spirituality (choice C) involves focusing on your ability to understand the world and how you can serve others. Exercise (choice D) is only one aspect of life that you can control to promote overall wellness.

4. **The correct answer is B.** The peak stage is the most contagious phase of the disease and when the symptoms are most intense. The incubation stage (choice A) occurs at the very beginning when an individual is capable of infecting others, but not as much as peak. Choice C is incorrect because the individual is least contagious during recovery. The prodromal stage (choice D) is the second most contagious stage.

5. **The correct answer is A.** Narcotics such as opium, morphine, heroin, codeine, and methadone are classified as opioids. These drugs relieve pain, cause drowsiness, and induce euphoria. Marijuana (choice B) is derived from the plant cannabis and is not an opioid. Phencyclidine (choice C) is a dangerous hallucinogen also known as PCP or angel dust and is not an opioid. Valium (choice D) is classified as a tranquilizer.

6. **The correct answer is C.** During aerobic exercise, the body can supply oxygen to all body parts. Choice A is incorrect because during anaerobic exercise, the body cannot be oxygenated fast enough to supply needed energy. Isometric (choice B) refers to static exercises that focus on resistance. Isokinetic exercise (choice D) focuses on range of motion through mechanical devices used to provide resistance.

7. **The correct answer is D.** Methane is a gas linked to air pollution and harm to the earth's atmosphere. Hydrogen (choice A), nitrogen (choice B), and argon (choice C) are gases that are naturally and abundantly found in the earth's atmosphere and do not harm the atmosphere in their natural states.

8. **The correct answer is C.** According to Kubler-Ross, there are five stages in the process of coping with grief and tragedy. The first stage is denial, or refusal to accept the facts or any information about the situation. Depression (choice A) is the fourth stage in grieving. Anger (choice B) is the second stage. Acceptance (choice D) is the fifth stage of grieving.

9. **The correct answer is A.** The hardening of the arteries is known as arteriosclerosis. Arthritis (choice B) affects joints, not the heart. Atherosclerosis (choice C) is the buildup of plaque on the inner walls of the arteries. Angina (choice D) is a condition in which the heart doesn't receive enough oxygen.

10. **The correct answer is B.** The onset of secondary depression can clearly be attributed to a traumatic event such as death or divorce. Choices A and C are incorrect because the onset of depression for no apparent reason that is often linked to brain chemistry is defined as primary depression. Choice D is incorrect because depression linked to the amount of sunlight an individual is exposed to is classified as Seasonal Affective Disorder (SAD).

11. **The correct answer is D.** Adults typically take in more calories than they expend, causing fat cells to grow to accommodate the increased intake. This growth of fat cells is known as hypertrophic obesity. The development of more fat cells typically seen in babies who are overfed (choice A) is known as hypercellular obesity. The idea that the body prefers to maintain its current weight (choice B) is known as set-point theory. Obesity due to genetic factors (choice C) usually relates to thyroid or endocrine issues or metabolism.

12. **The correct answer is C.** Transition occurs during the first stage of labor when the cervix dilates from seven to ten centimeters. This is the shortest and most strenuous part of labor. Choice A is incorrect because effacement, or thinning of the cervix, begins early in the first stage of labor. Choice B is incorrect because the thick mucus discharge called the "bloody show" is apparent before transition. Choice D is incorrect because the placenta is delivered during the final stage of birth, not during transition.

13. **The correct answer is B.** Blood alcohol concentration is determined by body weight, percent body fat, and gender. Choice A is incorrect because the type of drink is not as important as the amount of the drink ingested. Choice C is incorrect because the amount of food in the stomach will not alter the level of alcohol in the bloodstream. Choice D is incorrect because the time of day does not influence the BAC at all.

14. **The correct answer is C.** A sarcoma is a cancer that develops in connective tissue. Leukemia (choice A) is cancer involving the blood cells. Melanoma (choice B) is skin cancer. While a carcinoma (choice D) can occur in many types of body parts, it does not appear in connective tissue.

15. **The correct answer is B.** The major difference between barbiturates and tranquilizers is that barbiturates are designed to induce sleep, and tranquilizers are used to help cope during waking hours. Choice A is incorrect because both are addictive. Choice C is incorrect because, when used properly, both drugs are safe. Choice D is incorrect because both drugs are still prescribed.

16. **The correct answer is C.** There is no stage of distress in Selye's theory on stress known as General Adaptation Syndrome, or GAS, theory. Choice A is incorrect because the first stage of GAS is alarm reaction, which is a physical "fight-or-flight" response to stress caused by the surge of adrenaline. Choice B is incorrect because the stage of resistance is the second stage of GAS; it is the point at which the body reaches homeostasis with respect to adrenaline and energy levels. Choice D is incorrect because the stage of exhaustion is the third stage of the GAS theory. This is the point at which a stressed body becomes tired.

17. **The correct answer is C.** Fats are an excellent energy source and are denser than carbohydrates. Fats store energy for long-term use. While carbohydrates are also used for energy, choice A is incorrect because they provide a short-term energy source and are less dense than fats. Vitamins (choice B) are not a source of energy. Proteins (choice D) are not a readily accessible source of energy.

18. **The correct answer is B.** Progressive resistance, or isotonic, exercises employ the use of traditional free weights to provide resistance. Isometric exercise (choice A) focuses solely on resistance. Isokinetic resistance (choice C) involves exercising through a range of motion. Aerobic exercise (choice D) has to do with the amount of blood supplied to muscles throughout the body.

19. **The correct answer is C.** Down Syndrome, or trisomy 21, is a disorder in which there is an extra chromosome 21. This can be detected during pregnancy with amniocentesis. Diabetes (choice A) isn't detected by amniocentesis and usually doesn't develop in young babies. A cleft palate (choice B) is a physical birth defect, not a genetic defect. Hemochromatosis (choice D) is an abnormally high level of iron in the body and is not detected by amniocentesis.

20. **The correct answer is C.** Keeping noise at a reasonable level is a principle of motor vehicle safety, not a residential safety principle. Having a fire escape plan (choice A), changing the locks when you move into a new home (choice B), and asking for identification before repairmen enter your home (choice D) are all common residential safety principles. Other principles that fall into this category are installing a peep hole, keeping cooking and heating equipment in good working order, and storing poisonous substances away from children and pets.

DIAGNOSTIC TEST ASSESSMENT GRID

Now that you've completed the diagnostic test and read through the answer explanations, you can use your results to target your studying. Find the question numbers from the diagnostic test that you answered incorrectly and highlight or circle them below. Then focus extra attention on the sections dealing with those topics.

Health and Human Development

Content Area	Topics Covered	Questions
Health, Wellness, and Mind/Body Connection	• Dimensions of wellness, health, and lifestyles • Healthy People 2020 • Prevention • Mental health and mental illness	2, 3, 10
Human Development and Relationships	• Reproduction • Sexuality • Intimate relationships • Healthy aging • Death and bereavement	8, 12, 19
Addiction	• Addictive behavior • Alcohol • Tobacco • Other drugs • Other addictions	5, 13, 15
Fitness and Nutrition	• Components of physical fitness • Nutrition and its effect	6, 11, 17, 18
Risk Factors, Disease, and Disease Prevention	• Infectious diseases • The cardiovascular system • Types of cancer • Immune disorders • Diabetes, arthritis, and genetic-related disorders • Stress management and coping mechanisms • Common neurological disorders	1, 4, 9, 14, 16
Safety, Consumer Awareness, and Environmental Concerns	• Safety • Intentional injuries and violence • Consumer awareness • Environmental concerns	7, 20

Chapter 3

Health and Human Development Subject Review

OVERVIEW

- Health, Wellness, and Mind/Body Connection
- Human Development and Relationships
- Addiction
- Fitness and Nutrition
- Risk Factors, Diseases, and Disease Prevention
- Safety, Consumer Awareness, and Environmental Concerns
- Summing It Up

HEALTH, WELLNESS, AND MIND/BODY CONNECTION

Wellness is determined by overall health and vitality. Wellness is determined in large part by factors that you can control—such as diet, exercise, and your relationships with others. However, some aspects of health are out of your control, including age, gender, and genetic makeup. Understanding what you can and can't control helps achieve a feeling of empowerment, and empowerment is an important concept in overall wellness.

Dimensions of Wellness, Health, and Lifestyles

There are six dimensions to overall wellness: physical, emotional, spiritual, intellectual, interpersonal, and environmental. Each dimension is dependent on the others.

- **Physical wellness** includes not only the absence of disease but also fitness level and the ability to care for oneself. Physical wellness is determined by coordination, strength, and the five senses (sight, hearing, taste, touch, and smell).
- **Emotional wellness** reflects the ability to understand and cope with feelings or emotions. This also includes identifying any obstacles or factors that may affect emotional stability.
- **Spiritual wellness** involves developing a set of guided beliefs, principles, or values that give meaning and purpose to life.
- **Intellectual wellness** involves constantly challenging the mind and keeping it active. Continued creativity, problem solving, and processing information is essential for wellness.
- **Interpersonal wellness** is defined by the ability to develop and maintain healthy, satisfying, and supportive relationships with others. This includes participating in society in a positive way.
- **Environmental wellness** involves support from one's environment. The overall livability of the environment affects wellness.

Lifestyle choices include exercise, diet, and the choice to consume alcohol or use tobacco. People can influence their own lives by the lifestyle choices they make, but these four lifestyle choices play a major role in the leading causes of death in the United States.

Healthy People 2020

Healthy People 2020 is a nationwide program created by the United States Office of Disease Prevention and Health Promotion. Designed to promote health and wellness, this program began in the late 1970s and has been updated periodically to include new information and changes that follow society and societal needs. The 2020 initiative added categories that cover blood disorders and transmission of infectious diseases, along with global health and preparedness in response to recent global outbreaks of certain infectious diseases. Healthy People 2020 has also included sections on lesbian, gay, bisexual, and transgender health in response to our changing society.

Healthy People 2020 researches and responds to the leading health indicators in each time period, including biological, social, economic, and environmental factors that interact and affect how people maintain their health. It strives to improve population health, eliminate health problems, and increase health awareness for everyone. One of the main goals of Healthy People 2020 is the promotion of quality of life and healthy development for individuals of all ages by increasing healthy behaviors through education, awareness, and availability of health resources.

TIP: The national Healthy People Initiative aims to improve the quality of life for Americans. Its two broad goals are to increase the quality and years of healthy life for individuals and to eliminate health disparities among population groups in the United States.

The program focuses on prevention of disease, disability, injury, and preventable death, while also promoting healthier lifestyles. There are 42 topic areas that are covered, including substance use and abuse, heart disease, stroke, obesity, and mental health. One area that is seeing more attention is access to early and affordable detection and treatment. This initiative has found problems in availability, cost, lack of insurance coverage, and limited language access, all of which have led to an increased inability to access preventative services and delays or failure to seek needed care. These factors ultimately lead to higher costs in health care as lengthy treatments and hospital stays that could have been prevented with early detection and treatment result.[1]

Prevention

Healthy People 2020 seeks to increase awareness of prevention efforts designed to reduce the need for hospitalization and invasive treatment procedures. As people actively become more aware of healthy practices and incorporate them into their lifestyle, disease can be prevented. These healthy practices include regular well visits to the doctor and dentist, proper nutrition in diets, and exercise. Individuals need to meet the guidelines of the food pyramid and exercise regularly. It is important to discuss changes in diet and exercise with a doctor to ensure that there are no problems with the changes beforehand.

---

1 HealthyPeople.gov (n.d.). Healthy People 2020. Retrieved from: https://www.healthy people.gov/.

One form of prevention is through holistic health methods. **Holistic health** includes understanding the importance of all six dimensions of wellness. It includes good diet, proper exercise, adequate sleep, preventative care, moderation in alcohol consumption, and no drug or tobacco use. Behavioral changes are also important in creating a healthy lifestyle. **Holistic medicine** seeks to create an entire healthy being through body, mind, spirit, and emotion. A holistic practitioner is open to using different forms of healthcare prevention and treatment, including conventional and alternative methods. A visit to a holistic medicine practitioner for back pain might result in an examination of many different potential issues that could be causing the pain, including sleep position, stress, diet problems, and physical activity. An individual might leave the office with a prescription for medications to alleviate the pain but will also leave with suggestions of lifestyle modifications to help prevent the continuance of the back pain.

Holistic medicine operates under certain principles, including the presence of innate healing powers in all individuals. Because patients are people not diseases, treatment occurs through teamwork between the patient and the doctor. Treatment addresses all aspects of the patient and involves treating the condition not just the symptoms. Types of treatment could include patient education of lifestyle changes and healthy self-care practices, complementary and alternative therapies that could include reiki, homeopathy, aromatherapy, acupuncture, and massage therapy, to name a few.

Holistic treatment does include medications and surgical procedures based on traditional practices. The treatment professional could be a doctor of medicine, doctor of osteopathy, chiropractor, or homeopathic doctor, in addition to other holistic health professionals. Since there is such a wide variety of professionals involved, it is very important to check the credentials and reputation of any holistic practitioner before entrusting health matters to them.[2]

The **transtheoretical**, or stages of change, model is an effective approach to lifestyle management. The stages of change include the following:

- **Precontemplation:** An individual doesn't think he or she has a problem and doesn't intend to change.
- **Contemplation:** An individual recognizes he or she has a problem and intends to change in six months.

---

2 WebMD (n.d.). What is holistic medicine? Retrieved from: https://www.webmd.com/balance/guide/what-is-holistic-medicine#1

- **Preparation:** An individual plans to take action to change a behavior within a month or has begun to make a change already.
- **Action:** An individual outwardly modifies his or her behavior.
- **Maintenance:** An individual has maintained a healthier lifestyle for at least six months.
- **Termination:** An individual has exited the cycle of change and is not tempted to lapse back into old behaviors.

Mental Health and Mental Illness

People who are mentally healthy are comfortable with who they are and feel confident that they can meet the demands of life. When in a mentally healthy state, people are able to deal with negative feelings of disappointment, anger, jealousy, or regret in a healthy, constructive manner.

Abraham Maslow developed the **Hierarchy of Needs**, which suggests that most people are motivated to fulfill basic needs before moving on to more complex needs. The needs are arranged in a pyramid. As one progresses up the steps of the pyramid, the needs become more complex.

- The lowest level is made up of the most basic **physiological needs**, including food, shelter, sleep, clothing, and compensation.
- The next level is the need for **safety and security**.
- Next is the need for **love and belonging**, including social relationships, family, friends, and social interaction.
- Next is the need for **esteem**, including self-esteem, confidence, achievement, respect for others, and respect from others.
- The final level is **self-actualization**, which is the point at which individuals are finally doing what they are meant to do. This level includes morality, creativity, spontaneity, problem solving, lack of prejudice, and acceptance of facts. Maslow calls self-actualized individuals *transcenders*, or Theory Z people.

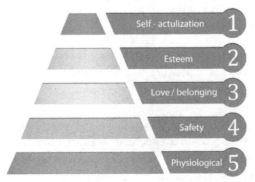

PYRAMIDS OF NEEDS

Responses to challenges in life influence the personality and identity of individuals. Psychologist Erik Erikson proposed eight stages that extend throughout an individual's lifetime. Each stage is characterized by a turning point or a crisis. One must master a stage successfully before being able to progress to the next stage.

1. The *first stage at birth year to 1* involves developing a trust that others will respond to your needs.
2. The *second stage from 1 to 3 years* involves learning self-control without losing the capacity for assertiveness.
3. From *3 to 6 years*, individuals develop a conscience based on parental prohibitions.
4. From *6 to 12 years*, individuals learn the value of accomplishment and perseverance without feeling inadequate.
5. In *adolescence*, individuals develop a stable sense of who they are based on needs, abilities, style, and values.
6. During *young adulthood*, individuals learn to live with and share intimately with others, often in a sexual relationship.
7. *Middle adulthood* includes doing things for others, such as parenting and becoming involved in civic activities.
8. *Older adulthood* includes affirming life's value and ideals.

Psychological Disorders

There are several types of psychological, or mental, disorders with varying degrees of severity: mood or affective disorders, schizophrenia, dissociative disorders, and somatoform.

Mood or affective disorders create emotional disturbances that are intense enough to affect the normal functioning of an individual. Electroconvulsive therapy is effective for severe depression, if no other treatments succeed. The three most common mood disorders are anxiety disorders, depression, and bipolar disorder.

- **Anxiety disorders** are mood disorders based on fear. They cause physical symptoms such as rapid heartbeat and tenseness.
  - **Simple phobia** is a fear of something definite, such as heights or closed spaces.
  - **Social phobia** is the fear of humiliation or embarrassment within a social setting. Shyness is associated with social phobia.
  - **Panic disorder** is the sudden and unexpected surge in anxiety and can lead to agoraphobia, which in its extreme is the fear of leaving home.

- **Generalized anxiety disorder (GAD)** occurs when worries push out other thoughts and a person cannot banish these worrying thoughts.
- **Obsessive-compulsive disorder (OCD)** includes irrational thoughts and impulses and the compulsion to do things over and over again. People with OCD feel out of control and embarrassed.
- **Post-traumatic stress disorder (PTSD)** is a reaction to severely traumatic events, such as physical violence, natural disasters, and accidents.
- **Depression** is the most common mood disorder and is an overwhelming feeling of worthlessness, despair, and sadness in such a way that reality is distorted.
  - **Primary depression** seems to start for no apparent reason and is usually attributed to brain chemistry. The most successful treatment for primary depression is antidepressant medication.
  - **Secondary depression**, also known as **reactive depression**, is brought about by a traumatic event. The most successful treatments for this type of depression include counseling and other therapies.
  - **Seasonal affective disorder (SAD)** is directly related to the amount of sunlight an individual is exposed to. This disorder worsens during winter months, and phototherapy is an effective treatment.
- **Bipolar disorders** are another type of mood disorder. People who swing between a manic state and a depressive state have a bipolar disorder. People who experience mania are often restless, have a great deal of energy, need very little sleep, and talk incessantly. Manic episodes vary in intensity; the "up" episodes of an individual with bipolar II disorder are more hypomanic in nature, rather than full-bown mania. Medications such as salt lithium carbonate can help prevent mood swings. Moods can also be stabilized with anticonvulsant drugs, such as Tegretol and Lamictal, which are generally used to prevent seizures.
- **Schizophrenia** has a number of symptoms, including auditory hallucinations, delusions of grandeur, persecution, inappropriate emotions, disorganized thoughts, and deteriorating social and work function. Schizophrenia is likely caused by a combination of genetics and environmental factors during pregnancy. Being born to older fathers or prenatal exposure to certain infections or medications can make an individual more susceptible to schizophrenia.
- **Dissociative disorders** cause a sudden, but temporary, change in identity or consciousness of an individual. Psychogenic amnesia is the inability to recall a stressful event, and psychogenic fugue occurs when an individual moves to a new place and assumes a new identity after a stressful event.
- **Somatoform disorders** are physical ailments without a medical condition to support them. Hypochondria is the belief that the person is sick when there is no medical evidence, and a conversion disorder is the unexplained loss of function of a body part.

HUMAN DEVELOPMENT AND RELATIONSHIPS

Over the course of a lifetime, a person will meet many people, have a variety of relationships, and live to see some family and friends die. Healthy living is the process of growing into a productive adult; coping with midlife issues; and aging and facing mortality in a positive, healthy way.

Reproduction

The sex organs necessary for reproduction are different for women and men, but arise from the same structures and carry out similar functions. The gonads of females are called the **ovaries**, and the gonads of males are called the **testes**. The testes and ovaries produce sex hormones (androgens, estrogens, and progestins) that trigger the development and function of the reproductive system. Within the gonads, germ cells develop into gametes (**sperm** in males and **eggs**, or **ova**, in females), which merge during the fertilization process.

The external genitals of the female are the **vulva** and the **labia majora** and the **labia minora**, which are two paired folds of skin. Inside these folds are the **clitoris**, the opening of the urethra, and the opening of the vagina. The external genitals of the male are the **penis** and the **scrotum**. The scrotum contains the **testes**, which keeps the sperm at a temperature five degrees below normal body temperature.

The biological sex of an individual is determined by the sperm that fertilizes an ovum at the time of conception. All ova carry an X-chromosome, and sperm carry either an X- or a Y-chromosome.

In females, progesterone and estrogen cause breast development, rounding of hips, and the start of the menstrual cycle. Maturation of the male reproductive system is about two years behind females. Testicular growth is the first sign of maturity. Body hair grows, the voice deepens, and height increases.

Conception and Infertility

The process of conception involves the fertilization of an ovum inside a woman by the sperm of a man during sexual intercourse. Once an egg is fertilized by a sperm, it becomes a **zygote**. As soon as fertilization occurs, the zygote starts the process of cell division, and moves through the fallopian tubes into the uterus. The cluster of growing cells forms a **blastocyst** that is implanted into the endometrial lining of the uterus. The blastocyst develops into a **fetus**.

Infertility is the inability to conceive a child after a year or longer of trying to do so. Most cases of infertility are treated with conventional medical therapies, such as surgery to correct anatomical problems or fertility drugs to help women ovulate. If these treatments don't work, assisted reproductive technology (ART) may be used. ART methods include intrauterine insemination, *in vitro* fertilization (IVF), gamete intrafallopian transfer (GIFT), and zygote intrafallopian transfer (ZIFT).

Pregnancy

Pregnancy is divided into trimesters of about three months each. Some of the major physiological changes to the mother and baby are as follows:

- **Mother:** During the first trimester, the uterus enlarges to about three times its nonpregnant size. During the start of the second trimester, the abdomen begins to protrude. The circulatory system and the lungs become more efficient. In the third trimester, the increased needs of the fetus put a strain on the woman's lungs, heart, and kidneys. The average weight gain during pregnancy is about 27.5 pounds. Preliminary contractions called Braxton-Hicks contractions start in the third trimester. In the ninth month, the baby settles in the pelvic region, and this stage of pregnancy is known as lightening.
- **Baby:** During the first trimester, the blastocyst implants in the uterus about four days after fertilization, eventually becoming an embryo at about the end of the second week after fertilization. The inner cells of the blastocyst are divided into three layers: One layer becomes inner body parts such as the digestive and respiratory systems. The middle layer of cells becomes muscle and bones, blood, kidneys, and sex glands. The third layer of cells becomes skin, hair, and the nervous system. An outermost layer of cells becomes the placenta, the umbilical cord, and the amniotic sac. These components provide nutrients and oxygen to the fetus. During the second trimester, the fetus does a great deal of growing, and it needs large amounts of food, water, and oxygen, which are all supplied from the mother through the placenta. During the third trimester, the fetus gains most of its birth weight.

Only about 3 percent of babies born have a major birth defect. The health and sex of a baby can be determined with several testing methods. These methods include ultrasonography, amniocentesis, chorionic villus sampling, and quadruple screen marker tests. **Ultrasonography** and **amniocentesis** are the most frequent methods used to detect fetal abnormalities. An ultrasound is done so that measurements of the developing fetus can be taken. A discrepancy in a fetal measurement can indicate an abnormality. Further detail can be obtained through amniocentesis. During amniocentesis, a needle is injected into the mother's abdomen to remove some of the amniotic fluid. The amniotic fluid contains all of the genetic material of the fetus, and so genetic, neural, and chromosomal abnormalities, such as Down syndrome, Tay-Sachs syndrome, spina bifida, and cystic fibrosis, can be detected. However, an amniocentesis will not show the severity of the abnormality.

Birth Process

The birth process occurs in three stages, and the whole process takes anywhere from about 2 to 36 hours. Labor begins when contractions exert pressure on the cervix and cause it to thin (efface) and open (dilate). The first stage of labor involves **effacement** and **dilation** of the cervix to 10 centimeters through contractions. The last part of the first stage is called transition and is characterized by stronger, more frequent contractions. The second stage of labor begins when the cervix is completely dilated to 10 centimeters and ends with the delivery of the baby. During the third stage of labor, the uterus continues to contract until the placenta is delivered.

Birth Control

Contraceptives are devices, substances, or techniques that are used to prevent pregnancy by preventing the fertilization of an egg or the implantation of a fertilized egg (ovum). Methods of contraception include the barrier method (condoms, cervical cones, diaphragms), intrauterine devices (IUDs designed to create an unstable environment in the uterus), hormonal methods (birth control pills and skin patch), natural methods (rhythm and withdrawal), and surgical sterilization (tubal ligation or tubal sterilization in women and vasectomy in men).

Sexuality

The sexual response in humans follows a specific pattern of phases: excitement, plateau, orgasmic, and resolution. Two physiological responses explain the genital and bodily reactions caused by arousal and orgasm. These are vascongestion (accumulation of blood in tissue) and muscular tension.

Any type of disturbance in sexual desire, performance ability, or satisfaction is referred to as **sexual dysfunction**. Some common sexual dysfunctions in men are erectile dysfunction, premature ejaculation, and retarded ejaculation. Female sexual dysfunction includes the lack of desire to have sex, failure to become aroused, and failure to achieve orgasm.

Sexual behavior is a result of many factors shaped by life experience and biological factors, and it is also influenced by gender identity. When a person's gender traits don't match his or her gender identity, that person is considered **transgender**. Transgender includes transsexuals (those whose gender does not match their gender identity); transvestites (those who enjoy wearing the clothing of the opposite gender); and intersexed, or androgynous, individuals (born without definitive sexual characteristics).

Most individuals engage in sexual intercourse as the ultimate sexual experience. Atypical sexual behaviors include fetishism, exhibitionism, voyeurism, sadism, masochism, and sadomasochism. **Paraphilia** is the term used to describe atypical sexual behaviors that cause harm to oneself or others. The use of force in a sexual relationship is a serious problem in human interaction. The most extreme forms of sexual coercion are rape, pedophilia, and sexual harassment.

Intimate Relationships

The first relationships formed outside the family are friendships. Friendships are based on companionship, respect, acceptance, help, loyalty, trust, mutuality, and reciprocity. Intimate partnerships are much like friendships, but these relationships include sexual desire, deeper levels of caring, and a greater demand for exclusiveness.

There are several stages of attraction between individuals.

- The initial stage of a relationship is defined as **marketing**, when individuals "market" their best selves while finding new friends and acquaintances.
- The next stage is **sharing of common values and beliefs**. If there is enough compatibility, then the relationship moves to the behavior stage.
- During the **behavior stage**, the relationship develops further into a friendship or a passionate love relationship.
- **Passionate love** is characterized by a temporary phase of intense feelings and attraction. This phase does not last very long and is often called infatuation or lust.
- Passionate love usually gives way to **companionate love**, which is a deep enduring attachment built on mutual support, empathy, and tolerance.

Friendship and marriage are based on many of the same characteristics of companionate love and the same level of deep commitment that strengthens over time. For most individuals, love, commitment, and sex are important parts of an intimate relationship.

Dating and Marriage

Most people in the United States find a romantic partner through dating someone who lives in the same region, is from a similar ethnic or cultural background, has a similar educational background, lives a similar lifestyle, and has the same ideas of physical attraction. Living together, or cohabitation, is one of the most rapid social changes in our society. Today, by age 30, about 50 percent of all men and women have cohabitated.

Sexual orientation in an intimate relationship refers to the gender that an individual is attracted to. There are three types of sexual orientation. Heterosexuals are attracted to individuals of the opposite sex, or gender; homosexuals are attracted to others of the same gender; and bisexuals are attracted to both genders.

The majority of Americans marry at some point in their life. Certain characteristics can predict whether a marriage will last; it is important that partners feel good about each other's personalities, have realistic expectations about the relationship, communicate well, agree on religious and ethical values, devise effective ways to resolve conflict, have an egalitarian role in the relationship, and have a good balance between individual and joint interests. Approximately 50 to 55 percent of US marriages end in divorce, a fact that is likely due to extremely high expectations of emotional fulfillment.

Starting a family can be stressful, but couples who keep their commitment strong after the arrival of a baby have three characteristics in common: a strong relationship before having children, planning their family and wanting children very much, and communicating well about feelings and expectations. As individuals become parents, there are typically four general styles of parenting, which vary depending on the levels of demandingness and responsiveness of the parent. The four parenting styles are as follows:

1. Authoritarian (high demandingness, low responsiveness)
2. Authoritative (high demandingness, high responsiveness)
3. Permissive (low demandingness, high responsiveness)
4. Uninvolved (low demandingness, low responsiveness)

Healthy Aging

Through good habits, individuals can delay, lessen, prevent, and sometimes reverse some changes associated with aging.

Midlife

In midlife, there is a general feeling of starting anew and coming to terms with mortality, although there is a slow decline of body function in terms of loss of bone mass, compression of vertebrae, loss of lean body mass, vision loss, hearing loss, fertility loss, and decrease in sexual function.

Many people retire in middle age, and their children are grown and leave home. These changes can bring about increased leisure time and changes in economic status.

Later Life

During the final stages of life, a greater emphasis is put on maintaining physical function and independence. **Life expectancy** is the average length of time that an individual can expect to live. Life expectancy continues to increase, which means more individuals are reaching older adulthood. This has increased the need for later forms of healthcare and chronic health issue management, both physically and psychologically. **Health span** refers to the length of time that one is generally healthy and free from serious disease. **Rehabilitation** is the return to normal functioning after an injury or illness. **Remediation** is the restoring of function through alternative methods. Government aid to elderly individuals includes housing subsidies, Medicare, Medicaid, and food stamps.

Death and Bereavement

Death and bereavement are a natural part of life and affect all individuals at one time or another. Death is the cessation of all body functions; the heart stops beating and breathing ceases. Life-support systems and respirators can sustain some body functions for a period of time, but if an individual does not regain independent breathing and heart functions, once life support is terminated, death occurs.

People prepare wills and other legal documents to express their wishes and dispense their estate (property and possessions) after death. Some people also leave instructions to donate their organs after their death, living wills that specify the medical treatment preferred in the event the individual cannot communicate his or her wishes, and orders not to resuscitate.

End-of-life care can be home care, hospital care, or hospice care, depending on the wishes of the individual. In some cases, when a patient is in a persistent vegetative state (unconscious and nonfunctioning) and cannot maintain normal body functions without artificial life support, life support is discontinued so as not to prolong life in a vegetative state. The practice of withholding medical treatment (such as feeding tubes and ventilators) that may prolong a life is called **passive euthanasia**. In **physician-assisted suicide**, the physician provides lethal drugs at the patient's request to end his or her life. **Active euthanasia** is the intentional act of ending the life of someone who suffers from an incurable and painful disease.

Based on Kubler-Ross' **Five Stages of Grief** (denial, anger, bargaining, depression, and acceptance), Charles A. Corr describes four main dimensions a person experiences while coping with a life-threatening illness: physical, psychological, social, and spiritual. Dr. Corr, a professor emeritus of philosophical studies at Southern Illinois University Edwardsville, has published extensively on the topic of death and dying and life and living.

Grief is a natural reaction to death or loss, and grief is present during the bereavement process. Psychologist William Worden identified four tasks of the mourning process:

1. Accepting reality
2. Working through pain
3. Adjusting to a changed environment without the presence of the deceased individual
4. Emotionally relocating the deceased and continuing with life

ADDICTION

The source or cause of an addiction can be the result of hereditary factors, personality, lifestyle, or environmental factors. Addictive behaviors are habits (usually bad habits) that are out of control and have negative effects on health and well-being.

Addictive Behaviors

Drug addiction is defined as the compulsive desire for a drug, the need to increase drug dosage, harmful effects to the addicted individuals and those around them, and psychological and physical dependence. **Physical dependence** is the most dangerous effect of drug use. A physical dependence means that the body relies on the drug for normal function. Removal of a drug from an individual who is physically dependent can produce significant withdrawal symptoms, which often include irritability, depression, physical pain, and death. **Psychological dependence** includes an intense desire to continue using a particular drug or drugs.

Drug habituation shares the same characteristics as drug addiction without the same level of compulsion or increased need of higher doses. Drug habituation is accompanied by psychological dependence but not physical dependence. Drug users can develop a tolerance to drugs so that they need an increased dosage to get the same effects.[3]

Alcohol

Alcohol, or ethyl alcohol (ethanol), is a form of a psychoactive drug. The concentration of alcohol in a particular drink is reflected in its proof value, which is twice the percentage of alcohol in the beverage. A standard alcoholic drink, referred to by the term "one drink," is 0.6 ounces of alcohol. As an individual ingests alcohol, about 20 percent is rapidly absorbed from the stomach into the bloodstream. About 75 percent is absorbed through the upper part of the small intestine, and the remainder enters the bloodstream later and farther down in the intestinal tract. Once it enters the bloodstream, alcohol induces the feeling of intoxication. The rate of absorption can be affected by the type of drink or the presence of food in the intestine. Food slows down the absorption of alcohol into the bloodstream, but carbonation or artificial sweeteners in the drink increase the rate of absorption.

Alcohol is metabolized primarily in the liver. **Blood alcohol concentration (BAC)** is determined by the volume of alcohol consumed over a given time period and by individual factors, including a person's sex, body weight, and percentage of body fat. Drinking low concentrations of alcohol can lead to

---

3 Engs, Ruth C. "Addictive behaviors," *Alcohol and Other Drugs: Self Responsibility.* Bloomington, IN:Tichenor Publishing Co. 1987. Used by permission of the author.

feelings of relaxation, joviality, and mild euphoria. Higher concentrations of alcohol lead to feelings of anger, sedation, and drowsiness and decreased internal body temperature. The effects of alcohol wear off slowly, and individuals often experience what is known as a hangover.

Drinking large quantities of alcohol over a short period of time can rapidly increase BAC levels to a lethal range. This leads to **alcohol poisoning**, which can result in death. Drinking alcohol in combination with taking illegal drugs is the leading cause of drug-related deaths. Alcohol crosses a restrictive layer of cells into the brain where it disrupts the function of neurotransmitters. This disruption creates many of the typical effects of drinking alcohol or drunkenness. With heavy alcohol consumption, these effects become permanent. Health problems related to chronic or excessive use of alcohol include diseases of the digestive and cardiovascular systems and cancers of the throat, mouth, esophagus, liver, and breast. During pregnancy, alcohol consumption presents health risks to both the mother and the developing fetus, and there is a strong chance of the baby developing fetal alcohol syndrome, an alcohol-related neurodevelopmental disorder. Alcohol abuse includes recurrent alcohol use that has negative consequences. Alcoholism involves more severe problems with alcohol use and a dependence on alcohol.

Tobacco

Smoking tobacco is the most preventable cause of poor health, disease, and death in the United States, but millions of Americans still smoke. Regular tobacco use causes a physical dependence on nicotine, which is characterized by a loss of control (cannot stop smoking), a buildup of tolerance to nicotine, and withdrawal symptoms in the absence of nicotine.

Tobacco smoke is made up of hundreds of chemicals, including toxic and poisonous chemicals such as acetone, toluene, and arsenic. When these particles are condensed, they form a brown sticky solid called cigarette tar. Cigarette smoke also contains carbon monoxide, a deadly gas that depletes the body's supply of oxygen.

Nicotine, the key psychoactive ingredient in tobacco, affects the nervous system and can act as a stimulant or a depressant. It stimulates the cerebral cortex of the brain, and it stimulates adrenal glands to release adrenaline. Nicotine inhibits the formation of urine, constricts blood vessels, accelerates heart rate, and elevates blood pressure. Other long-term effects of smoking are cardiovascular disease, especially coronary heart disease

(CHD); lung cancer and other cancers; respiratory diseases; stroke; aortic aneurysm; chronic obstructive pulmonary disease (COPD); arteriosclerosis (hardening of the arteries); emphysema; chronic bronchitis; ulcers; impotence; reproductive health problems; dental (gum) disease; and diminished senses, such as taste and smell. CHD is the most widespread cause of death among cigarette smokers and is often the result of atherosclerosis (plaque buildup in the walls of arteries).

Other forms of tobacco use, such as chewing tobacco, cigars, pipes, clove cigarettes, e-cigarettes, and bidis, also cause nicotine addiction and health issues. Oral tobacco use can lead to leukoplakia, the development of white leathery patches on gums, tongue, and inside of cheeks. This can be benign or a sign of cancer.

Environmental tobacco smoke (ETS), commonly known as **second-hand smoke**, contains high levels of toxic chemicals and poisons that cause headaches, sinus problems, eye irritation, and nasal irritation. Long-term exposure to ETS is linked to lung cancer and heart disease. Children and infants of parents who smoke are at greater risk of health issues. Smoking during pregnancy leads to an increase in the rate of miscarriage, stillbirth, congenital abnormalities, low birth weight, and premature births.

Other Drugs

Drug abuse is a harmful pattern of illegal or prescription drug use that persists in spite of negative consequences to health and psychological and social well-being. Dependence on drugs involves taking them compulsively despite any adverse effects that use might have.

Psychoactive drugs affect the mind and body function by altering brain chemistry. The properties of the drug and how it is used affect how the body or brain reacts to it. The effect of these drugs also is dependent upon user factors, such as psychological and physiological factors; and social factors, such as the social and physical environment surrounding the drug user. Psychoactive drugs include the following:

- **Opioids**, also called **narcotics**, or **narcotic analgesics**, are drugs used to relieve pain; they cause drowsiness and induce a state of euphoria. Opioids also reduce anxiety, produce feelings of lethargy and apathy, and affect the ability to concentrate. Some common opioids are opium, morphine, heroin, methadone, oxycodone, hydrocodone, methadone, and codeine. These drugs are typically injected or absorbed through snorting, sniffing, or smoking.

- **Central Nervous System (CNS) depressants** slow down the activity of the nervous system. They reduce anxiety and also cause mood changes, impair muscular coordination, slur speech, and induce sleep or drowsiness. Results of use can vary from mild sedation to death. CNS depressants include alcohol, barbiturates, and anti-anxiety drugs, also called tranquilizers or sedatives, such as valium and methaqualone. Barbiturates are used to help individuals calm down and sleep.
- **CNS stimulants** speed up the activities of the nervous system and cause an accelerated heart rate, a rise in blood pressure, dilation of the pupils and bronchial tubes, and an increase in gastric and adrenal secretions. Examples of some common CNS stimulants include cocaine, nicotine, and amphetamines (including dextroamphetamine, methamphetamine, and crystal methamphetamine), ephedrine, and caffeine.
- **Marijuana** used in low doses causes euphoria and a relaxed attitude. Very high doses cause feelings of depersonalization and sensory distortion. The long-term effects of marijuana include chronic bronchitis and some cancers. Using marijuana during pregnancy can impair fetal growth.
- **Hallucinogens** alter perception, feelings, and thought and can also cause an altered sense of time, mood changes, and visual disturbances. Hallucinogens include LSD (lysergic acid diethylamide), mescaline, psilocybin, STP, DMT, MDMA, PCP, and ketamine.
- **Inhalants**, which are present in a number of common household products, can cause delirium, loss of consciousness, heart failure, suffocation, and death. Inhalants can be categorized as volatile solvents (paint thinner, glue, gasoline), aerosols (sprays containing propellants and solvents), nitrites (butyl nitrite and amyl nitrite), and anesthetics (nitrous oxide).

Treatment of drug addictions include medication, self-help groups, rehabilitation and drug treatment centers, peer counseling, and counseling for family members.

Other Addictions

Drugs do not provide the only form of addiction. **Addiction** is basically a compulsive need for some habit or substance that creates physiological symptoms of withdrawal. Some alternate forms of addiction could include unhealthy attachments to food or excessive behaviors towards exercise, gambling, shopping, sex, online games, social media, and even bingo. In some way, the behavior becomes life-altering, and choices in lifestyle revolve around the addiction.

Gambling, bingo, and shopping can develop into addictions when the behaviors become compulsive. The individual can feel a sense of excitement and euphoria when buying or gambling—bingo is considered a form of gambling. This high is sought continuously, often leading to a depletion of earnings and savings, and often a descent into heavy debt, stealing, and lying. The individual can lose his or her family, job, and home in the pursuit of the euphoria associated with these types of addictions.

Sex addiction is not necessarily about the gratification of the physical act as much as it is about the initial excitement experienced during a first-time encounter, such as a first kiss. There is an unmet need for love and attention that the individual continuously tries to fill. Behaviors often include frequent and multiple partner interactions, which can result in an inability to form lasting monogamous relationships, and unprotected sexual activity, which can lead to contracting sexually transmitted diseases.

Some individuals engage in exercise to an excessive extent in an effort to satisfy an obsession over body image. The body is never perfect enough in the individual's mind, driving him or her to continue to exercise and seek excellence in performance. The high is experienced as endorphins are released during the exercise, and the individual continues to need this exercise in order to feel good about himself or herself. This addiction can lead to physical problems as the individual pushes too hard and causes strained muscles.

Online addictions occur as individuals spend inordinate amounts of time online either gaming or engaging in social media interactions. The high is from the interaction with the computer and often occupies long periods of time that should be spent working or taking care of normal daily routines.

FITNESS AND NUTRITION

Part of having a healthy lifestyle is being physically fit and eating well. Regular exercise and proper diet are important wellness factors.

Components of Physical Fitness

Exercise

Exercise lowers the risk of cardiovascular disease by lowering blood fat levels, reducing high blood pressure, and preventing arterial blockage. Exercise also reduces the risk of some cancers, osteoporosis, and diabetes;

boosts the immune system; improves psychological health; and prevents injuries and lower back pain. There are two types of exercise: **aerobic** and **anaerobic**. During aerobic exercise, oxygen is supplied to all areas of the body. During anaerobic exercise, the body cannot be oxygenated fast enough to supply energy to muscles from oxygen alone. This type of exercise involves a high intensity of effort.

Endurance training is a form of aerobic activity. It improves the function of chemical systems in the body and enhances the body's ability to utilize food energy. It includes exercises with continuous rhythmic movements, such as walking, jogging, cycling, and aerobic dancing. An indicator of the level of aerobic activity performed is the calculation of one's target heart rate, which is between 60 to 80 percent of one's maximum heart rate, which can be calculated by multiplying the maximum heart rate (220 – age) by .65 to .85.

The **Dietary Guidelines for Americans** recommend that children and adolescents should engage in at least 60 minutes of physical activity every day. Adults should take part in at least 2 hours and 20 minutes of moderate intensity or 1 hour and 15 minutes of vigorous intensity aerobic physical activity per week. Aerobic activity should be performed in segments of at least 10 minutes per segment and should occur multiple times throughout the week. Older adults should try to engage in the same level of exercise as younger adults, but, if health concerns prevent this, they should take part in as much physical activity as their conditions allow.

Physical activity should be appropriate to the individual's current level of physical fitness and should increase gradually based on health and ability. If an individual has health concerns, it is important to check with a doctor first to determine which types of physical activity will work best. Someone who is not currently active should not start out with a rigorous aerobic workout. It is important to be safe and go slowly.

In addition to health benefits, regular physical activity can provide a means of socializing with others, improve physical appearance, aid in sleep quality, increase energy, and provide more opportunity for independent living for older adults. A 45-minute walk during lunch can increase healthy physical activity and provide an opportunity to socialize with coworkers and friends. Many people set up step goals. The Dietary Guidelines recommend walking 10,000 steps a day.

There are five components to physical fitness:

1. Cardiorespiratory endurance
2. Muscular strength
3. Muscular endurance
4. Flexibility
5. Body composition

Cardiorespiratory endurance is the ability to perform prolonged, large muscle, dynamic exercises at a moderate- to high-intensity level. It increases the strength of the heart and certain related physical functions: the heart pumps more blood volume per heartbeat, the resting heart rate and resting blood pressure decrease, blood supply to tissue improves, and the body is better able to cool itself.

Muscular strength and endurance involves exerting force against significant resistance (weight lifting). Strength training should be done about two nonconsecutive days a week and should involve 8 to 12 repetitions of 8 to 10 different exercises. Strength training improves physical fitness and increases muscle mass, which means the body will require more energy to sustain life. There are three ways to improve muscle strength and endurance:

1. *Isometric exercises* are static and focus only on resistance (for example: pushing against a wall). It is difficult to measure the effectiveness of an isometric exercise, so they are not used often.
2. *Progressive resistance exercises*, or isotonic exercises, are those that provide a fixed amount of resistance, such as the use of traditional free weights.
3. *Isokinetic exercises* are those that include a range of motion and resistance provided by a mechanical source. The development of muscular endurance includes the ability to keep a specific muscle group contracted for a long period of time or to continually contract the same muscle group for a long period of time.

Flexibility is defined as the ability to move joints through a full range of motion. Flexibility depends on the structure of a particular joint, the length and elasticity of its connective tissue, and nervous system activity surrounding the joint. Stretching can help to provide flexibility and prevent injury when exercising and should include exercises for all the major muscle groups and joints. Muscle and joint injury can be treated with the R-I-C-E method: Rest, Ice, Compression, and Elevation.

A healthy **body composition** includes a higher proportion of fat-free body mass than fat mass. The proportion of fat-free to fat mass varies by age and sex. A higher concentration of body fat, especially in the abdominal region, can lead to health issues, including high blood pressure, heart disease, stroke, joint problems, gall bladder disease, back pain, diabetes, and cancer. Body composition can be altered by proper exercise and a healthy diet.

Regular exercise lowers the risk of cardiovascular diseases, cancer, osteoporosis, and Type II diabetes. Any exercise is better than no exercise, and benefits of exercise occur across all age groups and racial and ethnic groups. The more exercise an individual does, the more the individual realizes the benefits with stronger bones and muscles and increased lung capacity. Regular exercise with a steady progression can increase benefits, while minimizing risk of injury. Individuals should start slowly and increase and diversify their workouts as they go along.

Obesity

Many people exercise as part of a regimen to overcome obesity. Obesity can be caused by genetic factors or be due to the **set point theory**, which maintains that the body prefers to stay at its current weight, making it difficult for a person to drop below that weight. People who were overweight as babies may develop more fat cells, a condition known as **hypercellular obesity**, and this may make them more susceptible to being obese as adults. With the set point theory, there is more of an environmental influence as individual choices in food and exercise can influence how weight fluctuates. People who eat more calories than they expend have **hypertrophic obesity**, in which the fat cells expand to increase in volume and hold more fat tissue. People can remedy obesity through diet modification, physical intervention (appetite suppressants to control food intake), behavioral intervention (increased physical activity), or in extreme cases, bariatric surgery.

The prevalence of obesity has doubled among adults and tripled among children in the United States in recent decades. The easy availability of high-calorie, good-tasting, and inexpensive foods, along with larger portion sizes, have contributed to this trend in obesity. In addition to poor diet habits, technological advances and cutbacks in physical education programs in the schools have reduced physical activity in children. They do not develop good exercise habits when they are young, and this carries over to adulthood.

One way to measure body fat is through the **Body Mass Index (BMI)**. The BMI measures body fat based on height and weight and can indicate if an individual is underweight, normal, overweight, or obese. The healthy range of scores are from 20 to 25, with scores below 20 indicating that an individual is underweight, while scores over 25 indicate overweight and obese conditions. The BMI is calculated by dividing an individual's weight in pounds by their height in inches squared. This figure is then multiplied by 703. The BMI provides a guideline but is not completely accurate since it does not account for the variations in body type, height, and muscle mass.

Nutrition and Its Effect

There are about 45 essential nutrients that the body requires to maintain its maximum level of health and well-being. Food provides the essential nutrients and fuel that bodies require. The energy in foods is expressed in terms of kilocalories, commonly referred to as **calories. Macronutrients** include protein, fat, and carbohydrates, and each of these supplies energy to the body in differing amounts. Fat provides nine calories (kilocalories) per gram, protein provides four calories per gram, and carbohydrates provide four calories per gram.

Proteins are composed of chains of amino acids folded into a complex three-dimensional structure. Proteins form muscle and bone; are required for the production of blood, enzymes, hormones, and cell membranes; and are found in various forms in every cell of the body. Food obtained from animal sources (meat, eggs) provides complete proteins, but food from plant sources provides incomplete proteins. **Fats** are the best source of energy for the body and are stored in the body for long-term energy use.

Foods contain saturated or unsaturated fats or both. **Saturated fats** are solid at room temperature and generally found in animal products. **Unsaturated fats** generally come from a plant source and are liquid at room temperature. **Trans fatty acids** are unsaturated fats that have been altered so that their shape affects their behavior in the body.

Saturated and trans fats pose health risks, but some fats can be beneficial elements of a healthy diet. **Omega-3 fatty acids** are healthy polyunsaturated fats found in fish, nuts, and some plant-based foods like avocados. Omega-3 fatty acids reduce the tendency to form blood clots, inhibit inflammation, decrease abnormal heart rhythms, and help to reduce the risk of heart attacks, high blood pressure, and stroke in some people. **Carbohydrates** supply energy to cells and are the exclusive supply of energy for the brain and other parts of the nervous system and red blood cells. Carbohydrates are either simple or complex. Simple carbohydrates include sucrose, fructose, maltose, and lactose; these provide sweetness to foods. Complex carbohydrates are found in starches and dietary fiber; nondigestible carbohydrates in many plants. Fiber can help manage diabetes and high cholesterol levels and improve intestinal health. **Soluble fiber** turns into a gel in the intestine and binds to cholesterol to move it through the digestive tract. **Insoluble fiber** absorbs water and helps digestion.

There are 13 vitamins needed for proper nutrition and for proper maintenance of chemical and cellular processes. Four vitamins are fat-soluble (Vitamins A, D, E, and K) and nine are water-soluble (C and the eight B-complex vitamins: thiamin, riboflavin, niacin, B-6, folate, B-12, biotin, and pantothenic acid). Deficiencies in these essential vitamins can cause serious illness or death. Water is required to digest and absorb food, transport substances to different areas of the body, lubricate joints and organs, and help maintain body temperature. Water is found in almost all food sources.

There are also 17 essential minerals needed in a healthy diet. Minerals are inorganic substances, such as calcium, phosphorous, sulfur, sodium, potassium, and magnesium, that regulate body functions, help in growth and maintenance of body tissue such as teeth and muscles, and help in the release of energy from foods eaten.

Dietary Reference Intakes (DRI) are recommended intakes for essential nutrients that meet the needs for overall health and well-being. The Dietary Guidelines for Americans address the prevention of diet-related diseases (cancer, diabetes, cardiovascular disease). The Dietary Guidelines noted that while the rates of infectious diseases have decreased, the rates of diet-related issues have increased.

Roughly half of all American adults have been diagnosed with diseases related to poor eating and exercise habits. The Guidelines include the following recommendations:

1. Follow healthy eating patterns throughout life. Healthy habits are lifelong and should include maintaining a healthy body weight through nutritious foods.
2. Focus on variety, nutrient density, and amount. Individuals should choose nutrient-dense foods from all food groups while limiting calories.
3. Limit calories from added sugars, sodium, and saturated fats. It is important to limit foods high in refined sugars and sodium, including beverages, and cut back on foods containing saturated fats.
4. Move to healthier foods and beverages, including water.
5. Support healthy eating patterns in all settings.

By law, almost all foods require labels that break down the composition of the food into fats, proteins, carbohydrates, fiber, and sodium. Serving sizes have been standardized, health claims of particular foods are regulated, and dietary supplements must also have food labels. Individuals should limit intake of added sugars and saturated fats to no more than 10 percent of total calories each per day.

Sodium should be limited to fewer than 2,300 milligrams per day, and alcohol should be consumed in moderation (no more than one drink per day for women and two drinks or fewer per day for men). Some studies have indicated health benefits to drinking wine, yet it is not recommended that people who do not currently drink begin to drink as a result of these studies. A diet high in fruits, vegetables, and whole grains aids a healthy lifestyle. One rule of thumb is to create a plate of food that is comprised mainly of fruits, vegetables, and whole grains, with a little bit of meat or other protein.

RISK FACTORS, DISEASES, AND DISEASE PREVENTION

Infectious Diseases

In order to contract an infectious disease, several components are required: an agent, an entry point, a reservoir, and an exit point. A disease-producing agent—a **pathogen**—can be bacterial, viral, or fungal. The entry point can be either direct (bodily fluids, droplets, or fecal matter) or indirect (inanimate objects or nonhuman organisms, for example, mosquitoes).

There are four basic stages of an infection:

1. *Incubation* is the silent stage where symptoms are not apparent, but an individual is capable of infecting others.
2. During the *prodromal stage*, the pathogen, or disease agent, multiplies rapidly. During this stage, the infected individual (host) will experience some symptoms and is more likely to infect others.
3. During the *peak*, or *acme stage*, the symptoms are most intense; this is the most contagious phase of the disease.
4. The final stage is the *recovery stage* when the body begins to heal from the effects of the disease.

When a foreign organism infects the body, a complex system of responses is activated, two of which are the inflammatory response and the immune response. The immune system is the body's defense system against disease, and defense is carried out by different types of white blood cells, which are produced in bone marrow: **neutrophils** (travel in bloodstream to site of infection), macrophages (devour pathogens and dead cells), **natural killer cells** (directly destroy virus-infected cells or cancerous cells), **dendrite cells** (eat pathogens and activate lymphocytes), and **lymphocytes** (travel through the bloodstream and the lymphatic system).

Within the lymphatic system, lymph nodes filter bacteria and other substances from the lymph. When the lymph nodes are fighting off an infection, they fill with cells and become swollen. The location of the swollen nodes can alert doctors to the area of an infection.

There are three types of immunity that can fight off an infection.

1. *Artificially Acquired Immunity (AAI)*: Occurs when the body develops immunity from a vaccination or an infection
2. *Naturally Acquired Immunity (NAI)*: Occurs when the body itself fights off an infection and develops a "memory" for the infection to prevent reinfection
3. *Passively Acquired Immunity (PAI)*: Occurs when antibodies are used until the body develops a natural immunity against an infection

Bacterial infections can be treated with the administration of antibiotics that can kill bacteria. Vaccines can be administered to manipulate the immune system and cause the body to develop immunity to a certain infectious disease.

There are seven sexually transmitted diseases (STDs) that pose a major health threat:

1. *AIDS (Acquired Immune Deficiency Syndrome)*: Most serious and life-threatening sexually transmitted disease. AIDS is caused by the virus known as HIV (human immunodeficiency virus), which compromises the immune system by attacking helper T cells (CD4 T cells). HIV is spread through bodily fluids, such as blood, semen, and vaginal secretions, and it can pass from mother to baby. There is a great variation in the incubation time of HIV: from about six months to up to ten years. There is no cure for AIDS or HIV, but there are medicines available that can reduce the rate of destruction of helper T cells.
2. *Chlamydia*: Causes painful urination in both men and women. Most women with chlamydia are asymptomatic, but it can lead to pelvic inflammatory disease (PID) if left untreated. It increases a woman's risk of infertility and ectopic pregnancies and can lead to male infertility. It is the most widely spread bacterial STD in the United States.

3. *Gonorrhea*: Causes urinary discomfort in men and has a yellowish, green discharge. Most women infected with gonorrhea are asymptomatic, but some experience painful urination, vaginal discharge, and severe menstrual cramps. This STD is treated with antibiotics.

4. *Human Papillomavirus (HPV)*: Most common viral STD in the United States. About 6.2 million Americans are infected each year. Most people with HPV have no symptoms, and the virus can be cleared by the immune system without any treatment. However, if the infection persists, it can lead to genital warts (and common warts) and genital cancers, cervical cancers, penile cancers, and some forms of rectal and oropharyngeal cancers.

5. *Genital Herpes*: Infects about 1 in 5 adults in the United States, but most people don't know that they're infected. There are over fifty different herpes viruses, including chicken pox, shingles, and mononucleosis. There are two types of the herpes simplex virus: HSV-1 and HSV-2. HSV can be transmitted through sexual activity, including oral sex, and HSV infections usually last a lifetime. The virus can lie dormant for long periods of time and reactivate at any time. An infected individual is always contagious.

6. *Hepatitis B*: Causes inflammation of the liver and can cause serious and sometimes permanent damage. Hepatitis B is found in most body fluids and can be transmitted sexually, through intravenous drug use, and during pregnancy and delivery. Hepatitis B is similar to HIV, but it can spread through both sexual and nonsexual contact.

7. *Syphilis*: Caused by bacteria and can therefore be treated with antibiotics. After infection, an individual may be asymptomatic for four to ninety days.

Early diagnosis and treatment of STDs can help avoid complications and prevent their spread. Condom use is another effective way to help prevent the spread of some STDs.

The Cardiovascular System

The cardiovascular system consists of the heart and blood vessels. The heart pumps blood to the lungs through the pulmonary artery and to the body via the aorta. There are six major preventable risk factors for **cardiovascular disease (CVD)**: smoking, high blood pressure, unhealthy cholesterol levels, inactive lifestyle, obesity or being overweight, and diabetes.

CVD can be prevented by making dietary changes, especially decreasing fat intake (saturated and trans fats) and increasing fiber intake; getting regular exercise; avoiding tobacco; managing blood pressure and cholesterol levels; and developing effective ways of dealing with anger and stress.

Types of Cancer

Cancer can develop in all areas of the body. Treatment options depend on where the cancer is located, what type of cancer it is, and how far the cancer has progressed. Most cancers take the form of a tumor, which is a mass of tissues that serves no physiological purpose. Tumors may be **benign** (noncancerous) or **malignant** (cancerous). The spreading of cancer cells from one part of the body to another is called **metastasis**. The extent or spread of a cancer can be categorized into one of five progressive stages (stages 0 to IV). Malignant tumors are classified according to the type of cells the cancer is infecting.

- **Carcinomas** form from epithelial cells and account for 85 percent of all tumors. They can be in the skin, mouth, throat, intestinal tract, glands, nerves, breasts, genital structures, urinary tract, lungs, kidneys, and liver.
- **Sarcomas** are found in connective tissues, such as bones, cartilage, and membranes, that cover muscles and fat. Sarcomas account for about 2 percent of all cancers.
- **Melanomas** are skin cancers caused by prolonged sun exposure.
- **Lymphomas** are cancers of the lymph nodes or lymphatic system.
- **Leukemias** are cancers of blood-forming cells (bone marrow cells).
- **Neuroblastomas** generally affect children and start in the immature cells of the CNS.
- **Adenocarcinomas** are found in the endocrine glands.
- **Hepatomas** are found in liver cells.

Cancer is due to uncontrolled growth of cells because of genetics, exposure to mutagens, viral infection, and chemical substances in food and air. Dietary factors such as meat, certain types of fats, and alcohols can increase the risk of some cancers. Other risks include lack of exercise, obesity, certain types of infection, and exposure to chemicals and radiation. Diets that include a large variety of fruits and vegetables are linked to lower cancer rates. Also, self-monitoring and regular screening tests are essential to early cancer detection.

The following mnemonic devices are useful for self-monitoring and early cancer detection:

- The **ABCD test** for melanoma means checking a mole for asymmetry, border irregularity, color variation, and diameter greater than 6 millimeters.
- The acronym **CAUTION** promotes symptom awareness:

CAUTION ACRONYM	
C	Change in bowel or bladder habits
A	A sore throat that does not heal
U	Unusual bleeding or discharge
T	Thickening or lump in breasts or elsewhere
I	Indigestion or difficulty swallowing
O	Obvious change in wart or mole
N	Nagging cough or hoarseness

Cancer treatment methods include surgery, chemotherapy, and radiation. Lifestyle choices can greatly reduce the risk of cancer: avoid smoking, control diet and weight, exercise, protect skin, and avoid environmental and occupational carcinogens.

Immune Disorders

Immune disorders occur when the body comes under attack by its own cells (as is the case in cancers). The immune system often is able to detect cells that have recently transformed to cancer cells and is capable of destroying these cells. However, if the immune system starts to break down because of age, immune disorders like HIV, or chemotherapy, cells can grow out of control, often before the immune system can detect danger.

Another immune disorder occurs when the body confuses its own cells with foreign organisms. Some autoimmune disorders in which the immune system is too sensitive and attacks cells within the body include systemic lupus erythematosus and rheumatoid arthritis.

Diabetes, Arthritis, and Genetic-Related Disorders

Diabetes is a disease in which the pancreas does not produce insulin normally. **Insulin** is a necessary biological chemical that is used to process sugar in the body. There are three types of diabetes: Type I diabetes, which usually occurs during childhood; Type II diabetes, most often an adult disease; and gestational diabetes, a temporary condition during pregnancy. An individual with Type I will spend a lifetime monitoring blood sugar levels and injecting insulin. Obesity is a risk factor for Type II diabetes and can often be controlled through diet and exercise.

Rheumatoid arthritis (RA) is an autoimmune response that occurs when the immune system attacks healthy joint tissue. Symptoms of RA include stiffness, joint pain, swelling, redness, throbbing, muscle atrophy, joint deformity, and limited mobility. **Osteoarthritis** is caused by the wear and tear on joints and is usually a problem in older people. There is no cure for arthritis, but pain management and therapy can help.

Genetic disorders are diseases inherited from biological parents. The following are some common genetic disorders:

- **Hemophilia:** Passed from gene-carrying mothers to sons; the individual is missing factors needed for blood clotting
- **Retinitis Pigmentosa:** Eye disease that causes light sensitivity and the degeneration of the retina leading to eventual blindness
- **Color Blindness:** Affects the ability to discern colors
- **Cystic fibrosis:** Fatal condition caused by a defective gene prompting the body to produce a sticky mucus in the lungs and elsewhere

Stress Management and Coping Mechanisms

Stress can refer to two different things: the stressor and the stress response. The situation that triggers physical or emotional reactions is called the **stressor**, and the physical and emotional reactions are called the **stress response**. **Stress** is the general term used to describe the physical and emotional state that is part of the stress response.

Two body systems control the physical response to a stressor: the nervous system and the endocrine system. The autonomic nervous system consists of the parasympathetic division, which is in control when the body is relaxed, and the sympathetic division, which is activated during times of arousal. The sympathetic division triggers signals to tell the body to stop storing energy and to use it in response to crisis. This is carried out with the neurotransmitter norepinephrine. During times of stress, the sympathetic division of the nervous system triggers the endocrine system, where key hormones are released, including cortisol and epinephrine.

Hans Selye developed a theory of stress called the **General Adaptation Syndrome (GAS)**, which has three stages.

1. The first stage is the *alarm reaction* when the body encounters the initial stressor and initiates the fight-or-flight response, which is triggered by a surge of cortisol into the bloodstream.
2. The next stage of GAS is the *stage of resistance*. The body cannot maintain the levels of energy and adrenaline, so, in this stage, the parasympathetic division of the nervous system takes over and restores a state of stability called homeostasis.
3. The third stage of GAS is *exhaustion*. The stressed body will be tired at this stage because the initial adrenaline surge and the return to homeostasis expend a large amount of energy. Stress triggered by a pleasant stressor is called eustress, and stress triggered by an unpleasant stressor is called *distress*.

Behavioral responses to stressors are controlled by the **somatic nervous system**. Personality types also play a role in how an individual deals with stress. Type A personalities have a high perceived stress level and usually have problems dealing with stress. Type B personalities are less frustrated by daily events and other people's behavior. Type C personalities have difficulty expressing emotion and suppress their anger. They have an exaggerated response to minor stressors.

Stress can be managed in a myriad of ways, including having a good support system, improving communication skills, developing a healthy lifestyle, improving time management, and learning to identify and moderate individual stressors. Spiritual wellness can also help individuals deal with stress and improve overall health. Keeping a diary, changing unhealthy thought patterns, and using relaxation techniques that trigger a relaxation response are other ways to cope with stress.

A **relaxation response** is a physiological state that results in a slowing of breathing, heart rate, and metabolism; a decrease in blood pressure and oxygen; an increase in blood flow to the brain and skin and a switch of brain waves to the relaxed alpha rhythm. Counterproductive strategies for coping with stress include alcohol and tobacco use, drug use, and unhealthy eating habits.

Common Neurological Disorders

Two common neurological disorders are **Rett syndrome** and **Huntington's disease**. Rett syndrome affects brain development and is similar to autism. It is most common in girls. Development of affected individuals slows after 18 months, and children begin losing motor function.

Huntington's disease is characterized by the degeneration of brain cells in certain parts of the brain, causing loss of intellect, muscle control, and emotional control. A child of a parent with Huntington's disease has a 50/50 chance of inheriting the gene and developing the disease.

SAFETY, CONSUMER AWARENESS, AND ENVIRONMENTAL CONCERNS

In contemporary society, anxiety and even fear of random violence have become daily concerns for many. Learning simple safety procedures for the home and workplace can provide some sense of security. Being good healthcare consumers and protecting the environment are other areas of interest to many.

Safety

Many injuries are caused by the interaction of humans with environmental factors. The chief areas of safety concern are personal, residential, recreational, motor vehicle, and gun use. To maintain personal safety, one must think carefully, be aware of one's surroundings, and avoid atypical patterns.

Some common residential safety principles are to have a fire escape plan, install a peep hole, change locks when moving into a new home, and ask strangers such as repairmen for identification. The home can contain many poisonous substances that should be kept safe and away from children and pets. Home fires can be prevented by being careful about where smoking is done and keeping cooking and heating equipment in good working order. Always be prepared for fire emergencies with a fire escape route and smoke detectors.

Many injuries during recreational activities are the result of misuse of equipment, lack of experience, use of alcohol, or failure to wear proper safety equipment, such as a bike helmet or seat belt. Practicing motor vehicle safety includes keeping a mechanical vehicle in good working order, avoiding drinking and driving, driving defensively, giving pedestrians the right of way, and keeping noise at a reasonable level.

The proper handling and storage of firearms can help prevent injuries. People should know the gun laws in their state, never point a gun at an unintended target, keep fingers off the trigger, educate children, and keep guns locked away.

Intentional Injuries and Violence

Violence is defined as the intent to inflict harm on another person through the use of physical force. Social factors, such as violence in the media, and interpersonal factors, such as age, gender, ethnic background, and socioeconomic background, often contribute to violence. Alcohol and drug use often play a role in violent behavior as well.

Battering and forms of child abuse occur at every socioeconomic level. The issue with this type of violence is the need for the abuser to control other people. Child sexual abuse most often results in serious trauma for the child because the abuser is usually a trusted adult. **Rape** is a form of sexual assault that occurs when a person is forced to have sexual intercourse against his or her will. When a person is raped by someone he or she knows socially, it is considered **acquaintance rape** or **date rape**, depending on the level of the relationship between the attacker and victim. In a 2010 CDC Intimate Partner and Sexual Violence Survey, it was reported that most rape victims know their assailants: 51 percent of female victims were sexually assaulted by a current or former intimate partner, and 41 percent were sexually assaulted by an acquaintance. Of men and boys, 52 percent report being sexually assaulted by an acquaintance. **Sexual harassment** is defined as unwelcome sexual advances or other conduct of a sexual nature that have a negative effect on an individual or create an intimidating or hostile environment.

Consumer Awareness

In general, a person should seek the help of a healthcare professional for symptoms that are severe, unusual, persistent, or recurrent. When new symptoms first occur, there are self-treatment options that may benefit some individuals and certain health issues. When using self-medication, it's important to follow some simple guidelines:

- Read the label and follow the directions carefully.
- Do not exceed the recommended daily dose.

When seeking professional medical treatment, patients have the option of choosing conventional medical care or **complementary and alternative medicine (CAM)**. CAM practices are not part of conventional or mainstream healthcare or medical practice taught in US medical schools. CAM practices include traditional Chinese medicine (TCM), acupuncture, energy therapies, mind-body interventions, and herbal remedies.

Conventional medicine, also called **biomedicine** or **standard Western medicine**, is based on the application of the scientific method. Professionals who practice conventional medicine include doctors of medicine, doctors of osteopathic medicine, podiatrists, optometrists, and dentists. Healthcare in the United States is financed by a combination of private and public insurance plans. Medicare, Medicare Advantage, Medigap, and Medicaid account for 45 percent of patient coverage in the United States.

Environmental Concerns

Environmental health began with the effort to control communicable diseases. It has since expanded to include concern for air quality, global warming, and various forms of pollution, all of which play a role in some infectious and chronic diseases. Increased amounts of air pollutants are especially dangerous for children, elderly adults, and those with chronic health conditions. Some of the gases that are causing damage to our atmosphere and contributing to air pollution are carbon dioxide, carbon monoxide, chlorofluorocarbons (CFCs), methane, and nitrous oxide. Factors that contribute to poor air quality are heavy motor vehicle traffic, burning of fossil fuels, hot weather, and stagnant air.

The **greenhouse effect** occurs as thermal energy from the sun is trapped in the atmosphere by pollutants. This causes a rise in Earth's temperature that, in turn, causes droughts, ice melt, smog, and acid rain. In addition, the ozone layer that shields Earth's surface from the harmful UV rays of the sun is thinning and has developed holes in certain regions, including above Antarctica. Concerns for water quality worldwide focus on pathogenic organisms (bacterial, viral, or protozoan), chemical and hazardous waste, and water shortages, including shortages of clean drinking water. Land pollution is caused by landfills that release chemicals into the ground, pesticides, automobiles, accidental spills, radon gas, and nuclear reactors. Pollution also comes in the form of noise; loud and persistent noise can lead to hearing loss and stress.

SUMMING IT UP

- The six dimensions to overall wellness are physical, spiritual, emotional, intellectual, interpersonal, and environmental.
- The **transtheoretical model** is an effective approach to lifestyle management that includes pre-contemplation, contemplation, preparation, action, maintenance, and termination.
- Psychologist Abraham Maslow developed a pyramid expressing the **hierarchy of human needs**. According to Maslow, these needs move up the pyramid, starting with the most basic needs being **physiological**, then progressing to **safety and security**, **social relationships**, **self-esteem**, and finally, the highest level of need, **self-actualization**. Maslow called those who achieve self-actualization *transcenders*.
- Erik Erikson described eight stages of a human's lifespan:
  1. Birth to one year
  2. One to three years
  3. Three to six years
  4. Six to twelve years
  5. Adolescence
  6. Young adulthood
  7. Middle adulthood
  8. Older adulthood
- Types of **psychological disorders** include anxiety disorders, mood disorders, bipolar disorders, schizophrenia, dissociative disorders, and somatoform disorders.
- **Reproduction** refers to fertility, pregnancy, and various methods of birth control.
  - **Fertilization** starts the process of human development. **Infertility** can be overcome with several methods of treatment.
  - **Pregnancy** is divided into three trimesters, each lasting about three months. The birth process takes place in three stages.
  - The birth control methods that can be used to prevent unwanted pregnancies are **barrier method**, **intrauterine device**, **hormonal methods**, **natural methods**, and **surgical sterilization**.
- **Human sexual response** goes through the following phases: **excitement**, **plateau**, **orgasmic**, and **resolution**. Two physical responses to arousal are vasocongestion and muscular tension.

- Any type of disturbance in sexual desire, performance ability, or satisfaction is referred to as **sexual dysfunction**.
    - Common male sexual dysfunctions are erectile dysfunction, premature ejaculation, and retarded ejaculation.
    - Common female sexual dysfunction includes lack of desire to have sex, failure to become aroused, and failure to achieve orgasm.
- There are several stages of attraction between individuals: **marketing, sharing, behavior, passionate love**, and **enduring attachment**. Challenges that a relationship faces may include being open and honest, having unrealistic expectations, competitiveness, having unequal or premature commitment, balancing time spent together, jealousy, and supportiveness.
- The four general styles of parenting are **authoritarian**, **authoritative**, **permissive**, and **uninvolved**.
- **Healthy aging** is the process of growing into a productive adult, coping with midlife issues, and facing mortality in a positive, healthy way.
- Kubler-Ross proposed **Five Stages of Grief:**
    1. Denial
    2. Anger
    3. Bargaining
    4. Depression
    5. Acceptance
- **Addictive behaviors** involve habits that have become out of control. Factors leading to addictive behaviors include personality, lifestyle, heredity, social and physical environments, and the nature of the activity or substance.
    - **Drug addiction** is defined as the compulsive desire for a drug, the need to increase drug dosage, harmful effects to the addicted individual and those around him or her, and psychological and physical dependence.
- **Alcohol**, or ethyl alcohol (ethanol), is a form of a psychoactive drug. **Blood alcohol concentration (BAC)** is determined by the volume of alcohol consumed over a given time period and by individual factors, including body weight, percent body fat, and gender.
    - Health problems related to chronic or excessive use of alcohol include diseases of the digestive and cardiovascular systems and some cancers.
- **Nicotine** is the key psychoactive ingredient in tobacco. It affects the nervous system and can act as a stimulant or a depressant.
- Cardiovascular disease, especially **coronary heart disease (CHD)**, is the most widespread cause of death among cigarette smokers. CHD is often the result of atherosclerosis.

- **Psychoactive drugs** affect the mind and body functions by altering brain chemistry. Psychoactive drugs include alcohol, opioids, central nervous system (CNS) stimulants and depressants, marijuana, hallucinogens, and inhalants.
- The five components of physical fitness are **cardiorespiratory endurance, muscular strength, muscular endurance, flexibility,** and **body composition.**
- There are 13 vitamins, 17 minerals, and about 45 essential nutrients that the body requires to maintain its maximum level of health and well-being.
  - **Macronutrients** include protein, fat, and carbohydrates, and each of these supplies energy to the body in differing amounts.
  - Individuals should limit intake of added sugars and saturated fats to no more than 10 percent of total calories per day each.
  - Sodium should be limited to fewer than 2,300 milligrams per day, and alcohol should be consumed in moderation.
- In order to contract an infectious disease, **an agent, an entry point, a reservoir,** and **an exit point** are required.
  - The disease-producing agent is a **pathogen**. A pathogen can be **bacterial, viral,** or **fungal**.
  - The four basic stages of an infection are **incubation, prodromal, peak,** and **recovery**.
- The **immune system** is the body's defense system against disease, and defense is carried out by different types of white blood cells that are produced in bone marrow.
- Within the lymphatic system, **lymph nodes** filter bacteria and other substances from the lymph. When the lymph nodes are fighting off an infection, they fill with cells and become swollen. In the lymphatic system, there are two types of lymphocytes: (1) T cells and (2) B cells.
- There are **seven sexually transmitted diseases (STDs)** that pose a major health threat:
  1. AIDS
  2. Herpes
  3. Hepatitis
  4. Syphilis
  5. Chlamydia
  6. Gonorrhea
  7. Human papillomavirus (HPV)
- There are **six major preventable risk factors for cardiovascular disease (CVD),** including smoking, high blood pressure, unhealthy cholesterol levels, inactive lifestyle, overweight or obesity, and diabetes.

- **Cancer** is due to uncontrolled growth of cells because of genetics, exposure to a mutagen, viral infection, or chemical substances in food and air.
- **Autoimmune disorders** occur when the body comes under attack by its own cells.
  - ⊚ **Rheumatoid arthritis (RA)** is an autoimmune response in which the immune system attacks healthy joint tissue.
- **Diabetes** is a disease in which the pancreas does not produce insulin normally. Insulin is a necessary biological chemical that is used to process sugar in the body. The three types of diabetes are Type I, Type II, and gestational diabetes.
- **Genetic disorders** are diseases that are inherited from biological parents.
- The **nervous system** and **endocrine system** control the body's physical response to stress. Behavioral responses to stressors are controlled by the **somatic nervous system**.
- Hans Seyle's theory on stress is the **General Adaptation Syndrome (GAS)**, which has three stages:
  1. Alarm
  2. Resistance
  3. Exhaustion
- **Safety issues** include personal safety, residential safety, recreational safety, motor vehicle safety, and gun safety. **Violence** is defined as the intent to inflict harm on another person through the use of physical force.
- When seeking professional medical treatment, patients have the option of choosing **conventional medical care** or **complementary and alternative medicine (CAM)**.
- **Environmental health** includes concern for air quality, global warming, and various forms of pollution, all of which play a role in some infectious and chronic diseases.

Chapter 4

Health and Human Development Post-Test

POST-TEST ANSWER SHEET

1. Ⓐ Ⓑ Ⓒ Ⓓ	16. Ⓐ Ⓑ Ⓒ Ⓓ	31. Ⓐ Ⓑ Ⓒ Ⓓ
2. Ⓐ Ⓑ Ⓒ Ⓓ	17. Ⓐ Ⓑ Ⓒ Ⓓ	32. Ⓐ Ⓑ Ⓒ Ⓓ
3. Ⓐ Ⓑ Ⓒ Ⓓ	18. Ⓐ Ⓑ Ⓒ Ⓓ	33. Ⓐ Ⓑ Ⓒ Ⓓ
4. Ⓐ Ⓑ Ⓒ Ⓓ	19. Ⓐ Ⓑ Ⓒ Ⓓ	34. Ⓐ Ⓑ Ⓒ Ⓓ
5. Ⓐ Ⓑ Ⓒ Ⓓ	20. Ⓐ Ⓑ Ⓒ Ⓓ	35. Ⓐ Ⓑ Ⓒ Ⓓ
6. Ⓐ Ⓑ Ⓒ Ⓓ	21. Ⓐ Ⓑ Ⓒ Ⓓ	36. Ⓐ Ⓑ Ⓒ Ⓓ
7. Ⓐ Ⓑ Ⓒ Ⓓ	22. Ⓐ Ⓑ Ⓒ Ⓓ	37. Ⓐ Ⓑ Ⓒ Ⓓ
8. Ⓐ Ⓑ Ⓒ Ⓓ	23. Ⓐ Ⓑ Ⓒ Ⓓ	38. Ⓐ Ⓑ Ⓒ Ⓓ
9. Ⓐ Ⓑ Ⓒ Ⓓ	24. Ⓐ Ⓑ Ⓒ Ⓓ	39. Ⓐ Ⓑ Ⓒ Ⓓ
10. Ⓐ Ⓑ Ⓒ Ⓓ	25. Ⓐ Ⓑ Ⓒ Ⓓ	40. Ⓐ Ⓑ Ⓒ Ⓓ
11. Ⓐ Ⓑ Ⓒ Ⓓ	26. Ⓐ Ⓑ Ⓒ Ⓓ	41. Ⓐ Ⓑ Ⓒ Ⓓ
12. Ⓐ Ⓑ Ⓒ Ⓓ	27. Ⓐ Ⓑ Ⓒ Ⓓ	42. Ⓐ Ⓑ Ⓒ Ⓓ
13. Ⓐ Ⓑ Ⓒ Ⓓ	28. Ⓐ Ⓑ Ⓒ Ⓓ	43. Ⓐ Ⓑ Ⓒ Ⓓ
14. Ⓐ Ⓑ Ⓒ Ⓓ	29. Ⓐ Ⓑ Ⓒ Ⓓ	44. Ⓐ Ⓑ Ⓒ Ⓓ
15. Ⓐ Ⓑ Ⓒ Ⓓ	30. Ⓐ Ⓑ Ⓒ Ⓓ	45. Ⓐ Ⓑ Ⓒ Ⓓ

46. Ⓐ Ⓑ Ⓒ Ⓓ   51. Ⓐ Ⓑ Ⓒ Ⓓ   56. Ⓐ Ⓑ Ⓒ Ⓓ

47. Ⓐ Ⓑ Ⓒ Ⓓ   52. Ⓐ Ⓑ Ⓒ Ⓓ   57. Ⓐ Ⓑ Ⓒ Ⓓ

48. Ⓐ Ⓑ Ⓒ Ⓓ   53. Ⓐ Ⓑ Ⓒ Ⓓ   58. Ⓐ Ⓑ Ⓒ Ⓓ

49. Ⓐ Ⓑ Ⓒ Ⓓ   54. Ⓐ Ⓑ Ⓒ Ⓓ   59. Ⓐ Ⓑ Ⓒ Ⓓ

50. Ⓐ Ⓑ Ⓒ Ⓓ   55. Ⓐ Ⓑ Ⓒ Ⓓ   60. Ⓐ Ⓑ Ⓒ Ⓓ

HEALTH AND HUMAN DEVELOPMENT POST-TEST
72 minutes—60 questions

Directions: Carefully read each of the following 60 questions. Choose the best answer to each question and fill in the corresponding circle on the answer sheet. The Answer Key and Explanations can be found following this post-test.

1. Which type of psychological disorder is characterized as an affective disorder?

    A. Schizophrenia
    B. Stress
    C. Bipolar
    D. Somatoform

2. Which of the following is NOT a risk factor for heart disease that can be controlled?

    A. Weight
    B. Heredity
    C. Physical activity
    D. Hypertension

3. Which of the following are drugs derived from opium?

    A. Hallucinogens
    B. Tranquilizers
    C. Narcotic analgesics
    D. Barbiturates

4. What is the key psychoactive ingredient in tobacco?

    A. Acetone
    B. Toluene
    C. Arsenic
    D. Nicotine

5. Which of the following lists three of the five chief areas of safety concern?

A. Recreational, residential, personal
B. Recreational, fire, violence
C. Experience, personal, residential
D. Recreational, physical, violence

6. What is the term used for people who reach the highest level in Maslow's Hierarchy of Needs?

A. Achievers
B. Needy
C. Transcenders
D. Champions

7. The primary stage of Selye's General Adaptation Syndrome (GAS) is

A. resistance.
B. compulsion.
C. exhaustion.
D. alarm.

8. Which condition is a possible consequence of oral tobacco use?

A. Scar tissue
B. Swollen lymph nodes
C. Leukoplakia
D. HIV

9. Which type of stress is "good stress" according to Dr. Selye?

A. Distress
B. Eustress
C. Astress
D. Stressors

10. Which type of nutrient is the most calorie-dense?

A. Carbohydrates
B. Fats
C. Proteins
D. Fiber

11. Which of the following are fat-soluble vitamins?

    A. Calcium, magnesium, and iron
    B. A, B, C, and D
    C. A, D, E, and K
    D. B, C, and iron

12. Which of the following is an atypical sexual behavior that causes harm to one's self or others?

    A. Shared touching
    B. Transsexualism
    C. Paraphilia
    D. Masturbation

13. When referring to checking for melanoma, what does ABCD stand for?

    A. Abnormal, Blending, Color variation, Description
    B. Asymmetry, Border irregularity, Color variation, Diameter
    C. Asymmetry, Big, Color variation, Deformed
    D. Abnormal, Border irregularity, Color variation, Depth

14. What are the two forms of dietary fiber?

    A. Organic and inorganic
    B. Vegetable and mineral
    C. Soluble and insoluble
    D. Carbohydrate and fat

15. A vaccine can instill which type of immunity?

    A. Naturally acquired immunity
    B. Passively acquired immunity
    C. Artificially acquired immunity
    D. Actively acquired immunity

16. Which of the following hormones is responsible for breast development in females?

    A. Testosterone
    B. Progesterone
    C. Androgen
    D. Cortisol

17. What is the hormone cortisol secreted in response to?

A. Puberty
B. Release of ovum
C. Exhaustion
D. Stress

18. Which factor would be used to calculate your target heart rate for aerobic activity?

A. Weight
B. Body mass
C. Age
D. Muscle density

19. Which of the following refers to hardening of the arteries?

A. Arteriosclerosis
B. Atherosclerosis
C. Angina pectoris
D. Hypertension

20. What does HIV stand for?

A. Human immune virus
B. Human immunodeficiency virus
C. Habitual immunodeficiency virus
D. Habitual immune virus

21. Which of the following is best categorized as a way to ensure personal safety?

A. Wear a bicycle helmet.
B. Have a fire escape plan.
C. Avoid atypical patterns.
D. Drive defensively.

22. Which type of depression is best controlled by medication?

A. Primary depression
B. Secondary depression
C. Seasonal affective disorder
D. Loneliness

23. Which neurological disorder has traits similar to autism?

    A. Huntington's disease
    B. Rett syndrome
    C. Muscular dystrophy
    D. Neurofibromatosis

24. An agent or particle that causes disease is known as a(n)

    A. vaccine.
    B. antibody.
    C. antagonist.
    D. pathogen.

25. Which of the following is NOT considered an assisted reproductive technology (ART) treatment?

    A. *In vitro* fertilization
    B. Intrauterine insemination
    C. Gonadatrophin injections
    D. Gamete intrafallopian transfer

26. Amniocentesis can detect which of the following abnormalities?

    A. Diabetes
    B. Cleft palate
    C. Cystic fibrosis
    D. Phocomelia

27. Which of the following types of cancer develops in connective tissue?

    A. Melanoma
    B. Sarcoma
    C. Leukemia
    D. Carcinoma

28. Which type of specialist would be considered part of CAM healthcare?

    A. Dentist
    B. Registered nurse
    C. Herbalist
    D. Pharmacist

29. The five stages of grieving according to Kubler-Ross are

    A. denial, anger, bargaining, depression, acceptance.
    B. denial, pleading, grief, rage, closure.
    C. sadness, anger, grief, closure, moving on.
    D. sadness, crying, anger, closure, moving on.

30. Unwelcome sexual advances that have a negative effect on an individual is the definition of

    A. sexism.
    B. sexual harassment.
    C. sexual misconduct.
    D. rape.

31. Which of the following would be classified as a CNS depressant?

    A. Hydrocodone
    B. Cocaine
    C. Valium
    D. Ephedrine

32. Which of the following psychological disorders is linked to anxiety?

    A. Phobias
    B. Depression
    C. Schizophrenia
    D. Bipolar

33. Which dimension of health focuses on understanding self-purpose?

    A. Physical
    B. Intellectual
    C. Emotional
    D. Spiritual

34. Which is the most dangerous type of drug dependence?

    A. Physical
    B. Psychological
    C. Emotional
    D. Tolerance

35. What is the most basic level of need according to Maslow?

   A. Love
   B. Physiological
   C. Esteem
   D. Self-actualization

36. Which of the following is a symptom of physical dependence on a drug?

   A. A drug user gets a headache shortly after using his/her drug of choice.
   B. A drug user gets a headache after not using his/her drug of choice for a prolonged period of time.
   C. A drug user gets a headache while self-administering his/her drug of choice.
   D. A drug user gets daily headaches whether using his/her drug of choice or not.

37. Which of the following is one of the goals of the National Healthy People Initiative?

   A. Eliminate economic disparities among Americans
   B. Eliminate health disparities among Americans
   C. Focus on holistic health for all Americans
   D. Focus on making alcohol and tobacco illegal

38. Which of the following is defined as an interpersonal factor that may contribute to violence and intentional injury?

   A. Social factors
   B. Gender
   C. Violence in the media
   D. Address

39. What does set point theory propose?

   A. Dieting is a successful way to lose weight and keep it off without problems.
   B. Environmental factors are the strongest indicators of weight fluctuation.
   C. The body has a weight it tends to remain at making weight change hard to accomplish.
   D. Eating nutritious foods will lower weight and readjust the body.

40. Which of the following describes an authoritative parenting style?

    A. High demandingness, low responsiveness
    B. High demandingness, high responsiveness
    C. Low demandingness, high responsiveness
    D. Low demandingness, low responsiveness

41. Where is the primary site of alcohol metabolism in the body?

    A. Intestines
    B. Stomach
    C. Liver
    D. Kidneys

42. What would identify tolerance in someone who uses alcohol or other forms of drugs?

    A. Headaches when the individual stops using the substance
    B. The need for greater amounts of a substance in order to maintain the same feeling
    C. Sudden onset of depression or anxiety
    D. The compulsive desire or need for the drug

43. Which of the following best describes anaerobic exercise?

    A. Respiration of oxygen in the lungs
    B. Insufficient oxygen supply to reach all muscles
    C. Cardiorespiratory endurance
    D. Continuous rhythmic movements

44. When an individual believes that he or she is sick without any medical data to support this claim, this is known as a

    A. dissociative disorder.
    B. mood disorder.
    C. somatoform disorder.
    D. seasonal affective disorder.

45. How would a doctor initially check for the location of an infection in the lymph nodes?

    A. The doctor would need to look at an x-ray.
    B. The doctor would check for signs of heat.
    C. The doctor would have to run blood work.
    D. The doctor would look for swelling.

46. The initial stage of attraction between two individuals is

   A. behavior.
   B. sharing.
   C. marketing.
   D. mutual support.

47. Which type of fat provides health benefits?

   A. Saturated
   B. Trans fatty acid
   C. Hydrogenated oils
   D. Omega-3

48. The R-I-C-E method of treating muscle and joint injury includes

   A. rest, independence, compassion, and emotion.
   B. regular, intervals, conditioning, and endurance.
   C. rest, ice, conditioning, and endurance.
   D. rest, ice, compression, and elevation.

49. The cluster of cells that implants into the endometrial lining of the uterus is called a

   A. zygote.
   B. fetus.
   C. blastocyst.
   D. ovum.

50. Which type of white blood cell devours pathogens and dead cells as part of the body's immune system?

   A. Neutrophils
   B. Lymphocytes
   C. Dendrite cells
   D. Macrophages

51. Which STD is caused by an inflammation of the liver and can be transmitted through both sexual and nonsexual contact?

   A. Human immunodeficiency virus
   B. Human papillomavirus
   C. Genital herpes
   D. Hepatitis B

52. The most common viral STD in the United States is

    A. AIDS.
    B. HPV.
    C. HSV-1.
    D. HSV-2.

53. Which of the following best describes the greenhouse effect?

    A. Thermal energy is trapped in Earth's atmosphere by air pollutants.
    B. Sunlight is getting more powerful.
    C. Holes in the ozone layer allow more heat from the sun in the atmosphere.
    D. Many green plants are able to grow in certain regions of Earth.

54. Which of the following shields Earth's surface from the sun's harmful rays?

    A. Oxygen
    B. Methane
    C. Ozone
    D. Carbon

55. Which disease can occur when the pancreas does not produce insulin properly?

    A. Hemophilia
    B. Diabetes
    C. Huntington's disease
    D. Cystic fibrosis

56. What does the "U" stand for in the acronym CAUTION used to describe early detection of cancer?

    A. Unusual growths
    B. Unusual weight loss
    C. Unusual bleeding or discharge
    D. Unusual symptoms

57. Which of the following would increase the rate of absorption of alcohol into the bloodstream?

A. Drinking with a full stomach
B. Switching from beer to wine
C. Carbonation in the alcoholic drink
D. Heavier body weight

58. During which stage of labor is the cervix opened completely?

A. First stage
B. Second stage
C. Third stage
D. Postpartum stage

59. The most widespread cause of death among cigarette smokers is

A. cancer.
B. cardiovascular disease.
C. bronchitis.
D. chronic obstructive pulmonary disease (COPD).

60. Progressive resistance exercises are called

A. isotonic.
B. isokinetic.
C. isometric.
D. stretching.

ANSWER KEY AND EXPLANATIONS

1. C	13. B	25. C	37. B	49. C
2. B	14. C	26. C	38. B	50. D
3. C	15. C	27. B	39. C	51. D
4. D	16. B	28. C	40. B	52. B
5. A	17. D	29. A	41. C	53. A
6. C	18. C	30. B	42. B	54. C
7. D	19. A	31. C	43. B	55. B
8. C	20. B	32. A	44. C	56. C
9. B	21. C	33. D	45. D	57. C
10. B	22. A	34. A	46. C	58. A
11. C	23. B	35. B	47. D	59. B
12. C	24. D	36. B	48. D	60. A

1. **The correct answer is C.** Bipolar disorder is characterized as an affective or mood disorder. Schizophrenic disorders (choice A) are characterized by disorganized thought and distortions of reality. Stress (choice B) is a response to a change in environment, whether positive or negative, not a psychological disorder. Somatoform disorders (choice D) are physical ailments without a medical condition to support them.

2. **The correct answer is B.** An individual is not capable of controlling inherited factors, and some hereditary factors put individuals at a higher risk for heart disease. Weight (choice A) can generally be controlled through diet and exercise. Similarly, individuals can typically control levels of physical activity (choice C). Hypertension (choice D) can be controlled with exercise, diet, weight management, and medicine.

3. **The correct answer is C.** Drugs derived from opium are called narcotic analgesics. Hallucinogens (choice A) are either chemically synthesized or derived from mescaline (cactus). Tranquilizers (choice B) are sedatives produced synthetically. Barbiturates (choice D) are also produced by synthetic methods.

4. **The correct answer is D.** Nicotine is the key psychoactive ingredient in tobacco. Acetone (choice A), toluene (choice B), and arsenic (choice C) are poisonous chemicals found in tobacco smoke and not the key psychoactive ingredient in tobacco.

5. **The correct answer is A.** Many injuries are caused by the interaction of humans with environmental factors, and the chief areas of safety concern are (1) personal, (2) residential, (3) recreational, (4) motor vehicle, and (5) gun use. Choice B is incorrect because fire and violence are not categories of individual safety. Choice C is incorrect because experience is not an area of safety concern, although lack of experience can be classified as a concern when operating motor vehicles. Choice D is incorrect because violence and physical concerns are not individual safety categories.

6. **The correct answer is C.** People who reach self-actualization, the highest level of Maslow's Hierarchy of Needs, are called transcenders.

7. **The correct answer is D.** TThe first and primary stage of Dr. Hans Selye's GAS theory is alarm, also known as the fight-or-flight stage. Resistance (choice A) is the second stage in the GAS theory. Compulsion (choice B) is not a stage of the GAS theory. Exhaustion (choice C) is the third stage of the GAS theory.

8. **The correct answer is C.** Leukoplakia is a condition characterized by white patches on the tongue that aren't easily removed and are usually the result of excess oral tobacco use. Scar tissue (choice A) isn't a result of too much tobacco use. Swollen lymph nodes (choice B) are a symptom of an infection. Choice D is incorrect because HIV is a virus that can lead to the development of AIDS.

9. **The correct answer is B.** The term *eustress* refers to good stress on the body, such as during exercise or stress induced by the desire to do well at something. Distress (choice A) is usually considered "bad stress." The term *astress* (choice C) is not a psychological term. Stressors (choice D) are factors that can cause any type of stress.

10. **The correct answer is B.** Of the choices listed, fats are the most calorie-dense nutrients with nine calories per one gram of fat. Carbohydrates (choice A) and proteins (choice C) have seven calories per gram. Fiber (choice D) is a type of carbohydrate and has seven calories per gram.

11. **The correct answer is C.** Fat-soluble vitamins include A, D, E, and K. Choice A is incorrect because calcium, magnesium, and iron are minerals, not vitamins. Choice B is incorrect because the B vitamins and vitamin C are water-soluble. Choice D is incorrect because iron is a mineral, not a vitamin.

12. **The correct answer is C.** Paraphilia is any sexual act that causes harm to one's self or others. Shared touching (choice A) is usually done with mutual consent between two individuals. Transsexualism (choice B) refers to cases where an individual's gender doesn't match gender identity. Masturbation (choice D) is a form of self-stimulation and is generally not harmful.

13. **The correct answer is B.** The ABCD test for melanoma refers to checking a mole for asymmetry, border irregularity, color variation, and a diameter larger than a quarter of an inch.

14. **The correct answer is C.** The two forms of dietary fiber are soluble and insoluble. Both are derived from indigestible plant material. Choice A is incorrect because all fiber is organic material. Choice B is incorrect because fiber is not a mineral. Choice D is incorrect because all fiber derived from plants is a source of carbohydrates and fats are not fiber.

15. **The correct answer is C.** A vaccine is an injection of either an inactivated or a live virus that builds up immunity in the body. This is a form of artificially acquired immunity. Naturally acquired immunity (choice A) occurs when the body builds up its immunity after being exposed to a disease. Passively acquired immunity (choice B) is the process of using antibodies to develop immunity. Actively acquired immunity (choice D) is not a type of immunity.

16. **The correct answer is B.** Progesterone and estrogen cause breast development in females. Testosterone (choice A) and androgen (choice C) are responsible for genital development in males. Cortisol (choice D) is a hormone released in response to stress.

17. **The correct answer is D.** Cortisol is a hormone that is released in conjunction with epinephrine in response to stress. It is not a sex hormone that is elevated during puberty, making choice A incorrect. Choice B is incorrect because estradiol and LSH are released during ovulation. Choice C is incorrect because cortisol is released as a response to stress, not exhaustion.

18. **The correct answer is C.** One's target heart rate for aerobic exercise is calculated by subtracting age from 220 and then multiplying that number by a range of .65 to .85.

19. **The correct answer is A.** Arteriosclerosis is the hardening of the arteries. Atherosclerosis (choice B) refers to the buildup of plaque inside the walls of the heart. Angina pectoris (choice C) refers to chest pain caused by an insufficient amount of oxygen reaching the heart. Hypertension (choice D) refers to high blood pressure.

20. **The correct answer is B.** HIV is the acronym for human immunodeficiency virus, which is a virus that attacks the immune system.

21. **The correct answer is C.** Avoiding atypical patterns, especially after dark, is one way to ensure personal safety. Wearing a bicycle helmet (choice A) is best categorized as recreational safety. Planning a fire escape route (choice B) is a part of residential safety. Driving defensively (choice D) is categorized as motor vehicle safety.

22. **The correct answer is A.** Antidepressants are most successful in the treatment of primary depression. Secondary depression (choice B) is linked to a traumatic event and best treated by therapy. Seasonal affective disorder (choice C) is related to the amount of sunlight a person receives and is treated with exposure to UV light. Loneliness (choice D) is not a form of depression.

23. **The correct answer is B.** Rett syndrome is a neurological disorder, most common in girls, with traits similar to autism. Huntington's disease (choice A) is a genetic disorder in which there is a degeneration of brain cells. Muscular dystrophy (choice C) is a genetic disorder in which there is a degeneration of skeletal muscles. Neurofibromatosis (choice D) is a genetic disorder that causes tumors to grow in the nervous system.

24. **The correct answer is D.** Choice A is incorrect because a vaccine is used to prevent infectioA pathogen is an agent or particle that causes disease. A vaccine (choice A) is used to prevent infection. Antibodies (choice B) are used to fight against infection. An antagonist (choice C) is an adversary, not a particle or agent that causes disease.

25. **The correct answer is C.** Gonadatrophin is a fertility drug used to help women ovulate and administering injections of the drug is not considered an ART treatment. *In vitro* fertilization (choice A) is the process of fertilizing several eggs with sperm outside the woman's body and then reinserting them. Intrauterine insemination (choice B) is the placement of a man's sperm into a woman's uterus using a long, narrow tube. Gamete intrafallopian transfer (choice D) is removal of the egg from the ovary and mechanical insertion into the fallopian tube. Sperm is then added in hopes of fertilization. These three procedures fall under the category of ART treatments.

26. **The correct answer is C.** Cystic fibrosis, the fatal accumulation of too much mucus in the lungs, is the result of a genetic abnormality and can be detected through amniocentesis. An amniocentesis cannot detect diabetes (choice A), a cleft palate (choice B), or short limbs associated with phocomelia (choice D).

27. **The correct answer is B.** Sarcoma is cancer that begins in connective tissue. Sarcomas are very rare and only account for 2 percent of all cancers. Melanoma (choice A) originates in the skin. Leukemia (choice C) is a cancer that originates in the blood. Carcinoma (choice D) doesn't originate in connective tissue.

28. The correct answer is C. An herbalist would be considered a part of complementary and alternative medicine (CAM). A dentist, a registered nurse, and a pharmacist practice conventional medicine.

29. The correct answer is A. According to the process of grieving outlined by Kubler-Ross, the five stages of grief are denial, anger, bargaining, depression, and acceptance.

30. The correct answer is B. Sexual harassment is defined as unwelcome sexual advances or other conduct of a sexual nature that have a negative effect on an individual or create an intimidating or hostile environment. Sexism (choice A) is discrimination against an individual based on his or her sex. Sexual misconduct (choice C) is a more general term, whereas sexual harassment is more specific to the actions and language that are unwelcome. Rape (choice D) involves the act of sexual intercourse against an individual's will.

31. The correct answer is C. Valium is classified as a CNS depressant. It reduces anxiety and helps individuals calm down. Hydrocodone (choice A) is an opioid. Cocaine and ephedrine (choices B and D) are CNS stimulants.

32. The correct answer is A. Phobias are a psychological disorder linked to anxiety. CDepression (choice B) is an affective disorder. Schizophrenia (choice C) is a disorder linked to hallucinations and distortion. Bipolar (choice D) is an affective disorder.

33. The correct answer is D. Spiritual health focuses on the ability to understand one's purpose in the world and the ability to serve others. Physical health (choice A) focuses on physical wellness. Intellectual health (choice B) focuses on creativity and problem solving. Emotional health (choice C) focuses on the ability to deal with stress and conflict and to have emotionally appropriate responses to external stimuli.

34. **The correct answer is A.** Physical dependence is the most dangerous type of drug dependence; bodily functions become dependent on a drug. Psychological dependence (choice B) is a mental state and easier to overcome than physical dependence. Emotional dependence (choice C) falls into the category of psychological dependence. Tolerance (choice D) isn't a type of drug dependence.

35. **The correct answer is B.** Physiological needs such as food and shelter are humans' most basic needs. Choice A is incorrect because according to Maslow, love falls under the third level of need. Choice C is incorrect because esteem is the fourth hierarchical level of need. Choice D is incorrect because self-actualization is the highest level of need.

36. **The correct answer is B.** Headaches (and other types of physical pain) are a symptom of physical drug dependence, and these can occur when a user stops using his/her drug of choice. Headaches typically do not develop in the scenarios presented in choices A, C, and D.

37. **The correct answer is B.** The National Healthy People Initiative has two broad goals: to increase the quality and years of healthy life for, and to eliminate health disparities among, population groups in the United States. Choices A, C, and D are incorrect because the initiative doesn't focus on economic measures, isn't limited to a holistic approach, and isn't trying to eliminate tobacco and alcohol.

38. **The correct answer is B.** There are several interpersonal factors that contribute to violence: gender, age, ethnic background, and socioeconomic background. Social factors (choice A) are different contributing factors to violence. Violence in the media (choice C) is considered a social factor that contributes to violence and intentional injury.

39. The correct answer is C. Set point theory proposes that the body prefers to stay at its current weight, making it difficult for weight to adjust with diet. Choice A is incorrect because weight loss would be difficult to maintain. Choice B is incorrect because set point theory proposes genetic rather than environmental influences, which also makes choice D incorrect because nutritious foods would not influence the set weight.

40. The correct answer is B. An authoritative parenting style is one involving high demandingness and high responsiveness. High demandingness and low responsiveness (choice A) is characteristic of an authoritarian style of parenting. Low demandingness and high responsiveness (choice C) is characteristic of a permissive parenting style. Low demandingness and low responsiveness (choice D) is characteristic of an uninvolved parenting style.

41. The correct answer is C. Most alcohol is metabolized in the liver, not in the intestines (choice A), stomach (choice B), or kidneys (choice D). In fact, only about 2 percent of alcohol is excreted by the lungs, kidneys, and sweat glands.

42. The correct answer is B. Tolerance occurs as an individual needs an increasing amount of the substance in order to get the same feeling. Choice A is incorrect because headaches would be an indication of dependence and withdrawal. Choice C is incorrect because depression would be an indication of dependence and withdrawal. Choice D is incorrect because the need for the drug indicates addiction.

43. The correct answer is B. During anaerobic exercise, the body cannot be oxygenated fast enough to supply energy to muscles from oxygen alone. Choice A may seem like a good answer, but it doesn't relate to anaerobic exercise. Choices C and D describe aerobic exercise.

44. **The correct answer is C.** With a somatoform disorder, an individual presents physical ailments without any medical condition to support these ailments. Dissociative disorders (choice A) can cause a sudden, but temporary, change in identity or consciousness. A mood disorder (choice B) is itself a category of disorders. Seasonal affective disorder (choice D) is a form of depression.

45. **The correct answer is D.** The doctor would be able to determine the location of the infection by looking for swelling in the lymph nodes. Choices A and C are incorrect because there would be no need for an x-ray or blood work to determine the location. Choice B is incorrect because heat would not necessarily be present.

46. **The correct answer is C.** There are several stages of attraction between two people, and the initial stage is defined as marketing, during which an individual will "market" his or her best self. The behavior stage of attraction (choice A) is the third stage in which a relationship develops into friendship or passionate love. The sharing phase of attraction (choice B) is the second stage. Mutual support (choice D) develops in the last stage of attraction.

47. **The correct answer is D.** Omega-3 fatty acids provide health benefits, including reducing the risk of heart attacks. Saturated fats (choice A) and trans fats (choice B) pose health risks. Hydrogenated oils (choice C) are trans fats.

48. **The correct answer is D.** Muscle and joint injuries can be treated with rest, ice, compression, and elevation.

49. **The correct answer is C.** The cluster of cells that grows after an egg has been fertilized and implants in the endometrial lining is called a blastocyst. Choice A is incorrect because once the egg is fertilized by a sperm, it becomes a zygote. Choice B is incorrect because after the blastocyst implants in the endometrial lining, it develops into a fetus. Choice D is incorrect because an ovum is an unfertilized egg.

50. **The correct answer is D.** Macrophages devour pathogens and dead cells. Neutrophils (choice A) travel in the blood stream to the infection. Lymphocytes (choice B) travel through the blood stream and the lymphatic system. Dendrite cells (choice C) eat pathogens and activate lymphocytes.

51. **The correct answer is D.** Hepatitis B causes inflammation of the liver and can be transmitted sexually, through intravenous drug use, and during pregnancy and delivery. The human immunodeficiency virus (choice A) compromises the immune system and is spread through bodily fluids. The human papillomavirus (choice B) is spread sexually and can cause genital warts and certain cancers. Genital herpes (choice C) is transmitted through sexual activity.

52. **The correct answer is B.** The human papillomavirus (HPV) is the most common STD, infecting approximately 6.2 million Americans each year. Choice A is incorrect because although AIDS is an STD, it isn't the most commonly spread STD. Choices C and D are incorrect because herpes simplex virus 1 and 2 are not more common than HPV.

53. **The correct answer is A.** The greenhouse effect occurs as thermal energy from the sun is trapped in the atmosphere by air pollutants, which causes Earth's temperature to rise. Choice B is incorrect because the sun's effects on Earth may be getting stronger, but the sun is not getting more powerful. Choice C is incorrect because holes in the ozone layer contribute to a rise in Earth's temperature, but it is air pollution that causes the greenhouse effect. Choice D doesn't describe the greenhouse effect.

54. **The correct answer is C.** The ozone layer protects Earth's surface from the harmful UV rays of the sun. Choice A is incorrect because oxygen does not protect Earth's surface. Choices B and D are incorrect because in various forms methane and carbon are harmful to Earth's surface.

55. **The correct answer is B.** Diabetes is a disease in which the pancreas does not produce insulin normally. Hemophilia (choice A) is passed from gene-carrying mothers to sons. Huntington's disease (choice C) is characterized by degeneration of cells in certain parts of the brain. Cystic fibrosis (choice D) is a fatal condition caused by a defective gene prompting the body to produce a sticky mucus in the lungs.

56. **The correct answer is C.** The "U" in the CAUTION acronym stands for unusual bleeding or discharge, which is a possible sign of cancer.

57. **The correct answer is C.** Carbonation in a drink can increase the rate of alcohol absorption into the bloodstream. The opposite of choice A is true. Drinking on a full stomach can decrease absorption. Choice B is incorrect because the type of drink does not matter for absorption, other than carbonation or artificial sweetener. Choice D is incorrect because a heavier body mass will not affect absorption rate.

58. **The correct answer is A.** During transition, the cervix dilates to ten centimeters and is fully open. Choice B is incorrect because the cervix is already fully dilated in the second stage, and the mother pushes the baby out. Choice C is incorrect because the placenta is delivered in the third stage. Choice D is incorrect because the body begins to return to its pre-pregnancy state in the postpartum stage.

59. **The correct answer is B.** The most widespread cause of death among cigarette smokers is cardiovascular disease and in particular coronary heart disease. Although cigarette smoking is a primary cause of lung cancer and can cause other cancers, choice A is incorrect because cardiovascular disease is responsible for more deaths among cigarette smokers. Bronchitis (choice C) is a result of cigarette smoking, but it isn't a leading cause of death. COPD (choice D) is a result of cigarette smoking but is not the leading cause of death among smokers.

60. **The correct answer is A.** Isotonic exercises are progressive resistance exercises that provide a fixed amount of resistance. Isokinetic exercises (choice B) are those that include a range of motion and resistance from a mechanical source. Isometric exercises (choice C) are static. Stretching (choice D) is done to increase flexibility and prevent injury.

Like what you see? Get unlimited access to Peterson's full catalog of DSST practice tests, instructional videos, flashcards, and more for **75% off the first month!** Go to **www.petersons.com/testprep/dsst** and use coupon code **DSST2020** at checkout. Offer expires July 1, 2021.

Printed in the USA
CPSIA information can be obtained
at www.ICGtesting.com
JSHW012044140824
68134JS00033B/3247